Humour: A Very Short Introduction

VERY SHORT INTRODUCTIONS are for anyone wanting a stimulating and accessible way into a new subject. They are written by experts, and have been translated into more than 45 different languages.

The series began in 1995, and now covers a wide variety of topics in every discipline. The VSI library now contains over 500 volumes—a Very Short Introduction to everything from Psychology and Philosophy of Science to American History and Relativity—and continues to grow in every subject area.

Titles in the series include the following:

Noël Carroll

HUMOUR

A Very Short Introduction

OXFORD
UNIVERSITY PRESS

OXFORD
UNIVERSITY PRESS

Great Clarendon Street, Oxford, OX2 6DP,
United Kingdom

Oxford University Press is a department of the University of Oxford.
It furthers the University's objective of excellence in research, scholarship,
and education by publishing worldwide. Oxford is a registered trade mark of
Oxford University Press in the UK and in certain other countries

First Edition published in 2014

Impression: 9

Published in the United States of America by Oxford University Press
198 Madison Avenue, New York, NY 10016, United States of America

British Library Cataloguing in Publication Data
Data available

Library of Congress Control Number: 2013947882

ISBN 978-0-19-955222-1

Printed in Great Britain by
Ashford Colour Press Ltd., Gosport, Hampshire.

To Lorrie Moore,
comedienne extraordinaire

Contents

Acknowledgements

I am immensely grateful to the following people for the comments and suggestions that they have made with regard to this project. They include Joan Acocella, Aaron Smuts, Alex Orenstein, Jesse Prinz, Robert C. Roberts, John Deigh, Martha Nussbaum, Paul Woodruff, Nancy Sherman, Charles Nussbaum, Jenefer Robinson, Gregory Currie, Bence Nanay, John Kulvicki, Anna Riberio, Amy Coplan, Cynthia Freeland, Peter Kivy, Jerrold Levinson, Kathy Higgins, Mark Rollins, Stephen Neale, Alvin Goldman, Holly Goldman, Barbara Montero, Dan Jacobson, Zed Adams, Robert Stecker, Matthew Kieran, Stefan Bauman, Paul Taylor, Margaret Moore, Annette Barnes, Paloma Atencia-Linares, Barry Smith, and audiences at the University of Texas at Austin, Texas Tech, the University of Cincinnati, Rutgers, Marist College, SUNY Oneonta, The New School, Ohio University, University of Leeds, the London Aesthetics Forum, and the Graduate Center of the City University of New York. These people have sincerely attempted to temper my mistaken and self-destructive tendencies, but they have failed despite all their best efforts.

List of illustrations

A very short introduction

This is a book about humour—its nature and its value. Humour has been discovered in every known human culture and thinkers have discussed it for over 2,000 years. Predictably, the subject has attracted a massive literature. This book is designed to provide you with a brief entrée into that conversation.

Chapter 1 focuses upon the nature of humour. The leading theories of humour are reviewed in the hope that the contrasts that emerge between them will highlight important aspects of the phenomenon of humour. Ultimately, the chapter spends most of its attention on incongruity theories of humour, because incongruity theories (and successors thereof) are regarded as the most promising contenders by the majority of philosophers and psychologists.

An attempt is made to get at the nature of humour by defining comic amusement, the mental state that humour is meant to provoke. Definitional approaches are often frowned upon nowadays, but I would defend my attempt on the grounds that this method is the most fruitful one we have for flushing out the often hidden features of what we seek to illuminate. For even when our definitions are too narrow, we in effect learn of further aspects of the phenomenon.

I also believe that the incongruity theory, even if not fully adequate, provides us with a useful heuristic for future comic research by guiding us toward the kinds of variables we should attend to when investigating specimens of invented humour such as comic narratives. In this way, using the incongruity theory as a heuristic may pave the way for superior successor theories.

However, I have emphasized the incongruity approach not only for the benefit of theorists but also for the benefit of curious readers. For the incongruity approach provides one with an eminently serviceable method for discovering the secret to the humour one encounters daily in the form of jokes, comic asides, cartoons, sitcoms, and so on. Using the many examples of incongruity included here, along with the proposed theory, one can cut to the quick of the wit one hears and sees as well as garnering important clues about the way in which to construct humour on one's own. In that respect, the incongruity theory has immense, practical use value.

Chapter 2 examines the relation of humour to emotion and cognition. I begin by considering whether comic amusement is an emotion. This may seem to be an esoteric place to start. However, in recent decades very estimable advances have been made in the analysis of the emotions. Thus, by considering comic amusement as an emotion, we can exploit the insights of psychologists and philosophers of mind by exploring the ways in which comic amusement fits that model. By means of this framework we are led smoothly not only to an examination of the cognitive and affective dimensions of humour but also to a discussion of the importance of humour in terms of the service humour performs to vital human interests.

Chapter 3 concerns the relation of humour to value, specifically in terms of its social functions. Humour, and the comic amusement that attends it, has a crucial role to play in the construction of communities. It can serve as a disseminator as well as an enforcer of norms. But the social function of humour also raises certain moral questions, including: When is humour immoral? Is laughing at immoral humour itself immoral? Do the moral blemishes in an instance of humour render it less funny? These questions are especially pressing in our times where judgements of so-called political correctness are rampant and where many contemporary comics seem dedicated to responding to the forces of political correctness by pushing the envelope at an ever-escalating pace.

Chapter 1
The nature of humour

A Dubliner named Pat walks into a bar in New York and orders three shots of Jameson Irish Whiskey. He drinks them down and orders another round of three shots. And so on. Finally, the bartender asks Pat why he always orders his drinks in sets of three. Pat tells him that he likes to make believe he's drinking with his two brothers, who are far away—at present his older brother is in Galway and the younger one is in Sydney. In no time, Pat becomes a regular at the bar and every day, as soon as he enters, the bartender lines up three shots. But one day, as Pat bellies up to the bar, he says, 'Only two shots today.' 'I'm sorry for your loss,' says the bartender. 'What loss?' asks Pat. 'Well, you're only ordering two shots. Hasn't one of your brothers passed?' 'Naw,' says Pat. 'Don't ya know it's me; I'm on the wagon.'

If you find this joke funny, let us say that you are in a state which we will call 'comic amusement,' where the object of comic amusement is humour. That is, humour, such as that exemplified by the preceding joke, is what comic amusement is properly directed towards.

For our purposes, comic amusement is an emotional state. This is a contention that we will attempt to establish directly in the next chapter. But for now, grant us the supposition that comic amusement is an emotional state, like fear or anger, and allow us to show you what we can do with this assumption.

Emotions are appraisals directed at particular objects that are assessed in light of certain criteria of appropriateness and which cause certain phenomenological and/or physiological states in the subject undergoing the emotion. My fear is directed at a particular object, the tarantula in my sleeping bag, which creature satisfies the criterion of being dangerous; as such, I assess it negatively and this causes a chill to course through my being. Similarly, comic amusement is an emotion that is aimed at particular objects, such as the preceding joke, which meet certain criteria (to be discussed), where such appraisals then eventuate in enjoyment and an experience of levity which itself correlates with increased activation of the reward network of the limbic system in the brain. The general name for all those objects that give rise to comic amusement is humour. That is what we meant earlier when we said that humour is the object of comic emotion.

The word 'humour' comes from the Latin *humor*, which means liquid or fluid, including bodily fluids. Ancient physicians maintained that one's well-being depended upon a balance between four such fluids: blood, phlegm, black bile, and yellow bile. Where these bodily fluids are disproportioned, various personality traits become pronounced; an excess of blood, for example, makes one sanguine or hopeful. In this way, 'humour' became associated with the idea of a person whose temperament deviates from the norm. Such people were regarded as eccentric; by the 16th century they were seen as ridiculous and, thereby, a fit subject for mimicking by comic actors. As a result, 'humour' evolved into what *humour*ists did.

(Interestingly, *zaniness* underwent a similar etymological fate. It began as a label for clownish imitators and then evolved into a quality in its own right.)

In any case, humour is a pervasive feature of human life. We find it everywhere—at work and at play, in private and public affairs. Sometimes we make it ourselves; often we pay others to create it for us, including playwrights, novelists, film-makers, stand-up comics, clowns, and so on. According to some, such as Rabelais, humour is distinctively human, a property of our species and no other, although some scientists have claimed that certain chimpanzees that had been taught sign language traded puns and enjoyed them. But even if it is not the case that humour is a uniquely human invention, it seems to be a nearly universal component of human societies. Thus it should come as no surprise that it has been a perennial topic for speculation, especially on the part of thinkers ambitious enough to attempt to comment on every facet of human life.

In his *Philebus*, Plato asserts that the laughter that attends humour is directed at vice, particularly at the vice of self-unawareness. That is, we laugh at people who fail to follow the Socratic adage 'Know thyself,' and who instead deceive themselves, imagining that they are wiser than they are, or stronger, or taller, or braver. Thus, for Plato, amusement contains an element of malice.

In his *Republic*, Plato expresses his distrust of humour. He feared that it could lead to bouts of what Homer calls 'unquenchable laughter,' and, of course, Plato was suspicious of anything that contributed to a lack of rational self-control. For this reason, he discouraged the cultivation of laughter in the guardian class of his Republic and urged that they not be exposed to representations of gods and heroes laughing.

Like his mentor Plato, Aristotle defines humour as a form of abuse. In his *Poetics*, he conjectures that comedy began as invective, perhaps as a Greek version of today's African-American practice of competitive insults such as the Toast, the Dozens, and Yo' Momma (as in 'Yo' Momma is so fat, she needs two zip codes').

Aristotle maintained that theatrical comedy of his own day involved the portrayal of people as worse than average.

However, unlike Plato, Aristotle reserves a place for humour in the virtuous life, since such a life should involve playful relaxation as a counterweight to activity. In his *Nicomachean Ethics*, he recommends that the witty person of taste strike the mean between the excessive jocularity of the buffoon, on the one hand, and the lack of humour of the boor, on the other hand. Moreover, Aristotle cautions, the laughter of the virtuous person must be tactful and moderate. Aristotle agrees with Plato that laughter can get out of hand. Thus he warns the virtuous against the danger of buffoonery—an inability to resist the temptation to provoke laughter, no matter what the occasion and whatever the means required. Such a person could scarcely be regarded as a reliable citizen.

A similar distrust of humour may be found in Epictetus and the Stoics who, like Plato, placed a premium on emotional self-control, while Church fathers such as Ambrose and Jerome assimilated the Stoic suspicion of laughter, despite the fact that Jesus himself appears to have valued it.

As the list of notables already mentioned indicates, humour is a topic that has been broached by many distinguished thinkers, including not only those named so far but also Descartes, Pascal, Hobbes, Kant, Hegel, Hazlitt, Schopenhauer, Kierkegaard, Freud, Bergson, and Koestler, to name a few. Certain recurring theoretical approaches to humour have emerged from their writings. And the best way to get at the nature of the beast is to survey the strengths and weaknesses of some of the available theories of humour.

Theories of humour

As already indicated, humour is the object of comic amusement, properly so called. Thus one way to illuminate the nature of humour is to analyse what it takes to give rise to the emotional state of comic amusement, and work backwards from there. Humour, then, will comprise those features of the objects of comic amusement that account for the provocation of that state.

The leading theories of that which engenders comic amusement are the superiority theory, the incongruity theory, the release theory, the play theory, and the dispositional theory. In this section, these are the approaches we will survey. Since I, like most philosophers and psychologists, find the incongruity theory (or some variation thereof) to be the most fruitful of these five hypotheses, I will spend the greater part of my energies expounding and defending a version of that theory. Emphasis on the incongruity theory is further justified, moreover, because it will afford readers a generally effective means for analysing comic structures that they encounter every day and which range from jokes to comic plots.

The superiority theory

The association—found in Plato and Aristotle—of humour with malice and abuse towards people marked as deficient suggests what has been called the *superiority theory* of humour, which was articulated in its most compact form by Thomas Hobbes. In his *Leviathan*, Hobbes identifies comic amusement with 'sudden glory' and says it is 'the passion which makes those grimaces called laughter; and is caused either by some sudden act of their own, that pleases them, or by the apprehension of some deformed thing in another, by comparison whereof they suddenly applaud themselves.' For Hobbes, the feeling humour stokes is that of the pleasure of finding oneself superior to others, along with contempt for them. In the view of a superiority theorist such as Hobbes, we laugh at the character of the Irishman Pat in our opening joke because he is either incredibly stupid or self-deceived.

That is, according to Hobbes, laughter results from perceiving infirmities in others which reinforce our own sense of superiority.

Hobbes adds that the object of humour may also be our former selves, in order to accommodate the fact that we sometimes laugh at ourselves. But when we laugh at ourselves for some incredibly dumb behaviour—say, putting shaving cream on our toothbrush—we do so putatively from a present perspective of superior insight that sees and savours the ridiculous absentmindedness of the person we once were.

Another famous superiority theorist was Charles Baudelaire, who regarded the malice inherent in the comic as the clearest token of the satanic in human beings.

There is a lot to be said for the superiority theory of humour. Much humour is undeniably at the expense of characters who are particularly stupid, vain, greedy, cruel, ruthless, dirty, lubricious, and deficient in other respects. Consider, for example: Polish and Italian jokes as told by Irish-Americans; Irish jokes as told by the English; Belgian jokes by the French; Chelm jokes by Jews; Russian jokes by Poles; Ukrainian jokes by Russians; Portuguese jokes as told by Brazilians; Newfie jokes by other Canadians; and Sikh jokes by Indians—not to mention blonde jokes, told by anyone. These are all essentially 'moron jokes;' they can all be retold by asking, 'Why did the moron do X?' or 'How does the moron do X?' But moron jokes are aimed at such monumental lapses in intelligence to which virtually anyone can feel superior.

Similarly, many jokes are told at the expense of people with physical disabilities (e.g. stuttering) or cultural disadvantages (e.g. illiteracy) and from an implicit position of superiority. What the superiority theory asserts is that we find the comic butts in such humour not merely different from us but also inferior to us.

Likewise, practical jokes aim at humiliating their targets, thereby asserting the one-upmanship of the perpetrator of the trick. Even most verbal jokes bear a similar taint inasmuch as the jokester inveigles the listener into embracing an absurdity—the typically nonsensical interpretation of the punchline that we need to infer in order for the joke to take hold. For the superiority theorist, the laughter of comic amusement is aggressive. Indeed, in the early 20th century, the superiority theorist A.M. Ludovici thought as much could be derived from the very image of laughter, where the very gesture itself, baring as it does the teeth, is a form of ritual biting, and, therefore, of hostility.

Many jokes appear to celebrate the superiority of the tellers and the listeners by featuring a comic butt who is outsmarted in the story world of the joke, as in this Welsh joke at Gordon Brown's expense:

> During his tenure as prime minister, Gordon Brown was visiting a primary school in Wales. He attended a class that was discussing the meaning of words. The teacher asked Mr Brown to discuss the meaning of the word 'tragedy.'
> Mr Brown began by asking for examples of what would count as tragedies. One boy offered: 'If my friend who lives on a farm was playing in the fields and was run over by a tractor and killed, that would be a tragedy.'
> Gordon Brown replied: 'No, that would be an accident.'
> A girl in the first row said: 'If a school bus with fifty children ran over a cliff and they were all killed, that would be a tragedy.'
> But Mr Brown replied: 'No, that would be a great loss.'
> Finally a boy in the back row of the class suggested: 'If a plane carrying Chancellor Darling were shot to pieces by a SCUD rocket, that would be a tragedy.'
> 'Good,' said Gordon Brown, adding, 'but why would it be a tragedy?'
> 'Well,' the boy answered, 'because it wouldn't be a great loss and it probably wasn't an accident either.'

In jokes like these, tellers and listeners alike feel they've gotten one up on the former prime minister. However, a sense of superiority can also obtain in jokes where we bear no animus towards their butts but only amusement at their ignorance.

For example:

> Two Scottish nuns are traveling to the United States. One of the sisters tells the other: 'You know, in America they eat dogs.'
>
> Their plane lands in JFK and they take a cab to Manhattan. No sooner do they get settled in their convent than they take a walk. Sighting a hot-dog stand, they order two hot dogs. The first sister takes hers out of the wrapping, looks at it and asks the other nun: 'What part did you get?'

The superiority theory has the virtue of handling a great deal of data, from laughter at moron jokes to laughter at people slipping on the ice (i.e. people clumsier than we are). Much laughter is nasty, directed at foolishness, and the superiority theory ostensibly explains why this is so. Here, laughter is a sign of pleasure, and the pleasure we take in the foolishness of others is putatively the recognition that we are better than they are.

However, despite the explanatory reach of the superiority theory, it suffers notable limitations. Feelings of superiority cannot be a necessary condition for laughter, since there are many cases of laughter that do not involve them. For example, we laugh at word wit such as puns with no tendentious edge, such as: 'What do you call it when you dynamite the kitchen?' 'Linoleum blown apart.' However, when we laugh in these cases, it is far from clear to whom one feels superior, or in what way the utterers of such word wit are inferior to us. Indeed, they may strike us as being cleverer than we are.

In addition, we may laugh when we are amiably teased but this is hard to explain in terms of feelings of superiority we supposedly have, since it is not some former self whose shortcomings are being tweaked but ourselves in the present. Likewise, we often laugh at ourselves precisely at the moment when we find that we are in the process of doing something foolish, such as putting sugar instead of parmesan cheese on our spaghetti when we are tired. In that case, we are not laughing at some former self but at the guy with the spaghetti in his mouth.

The superiority theory is also difficult to square with self-deprecatory humour. Undoubtedly, it will be suggested that this kind of humour is not hard to understand, since listeners will feel superior to the person who is running himself down. But the mystery here lies elsewhere. The question is: Why does the perpetrator of self-deprecatory humour find it funny? Perhaps it will be said that someone like Woody Allen enjoys this genre because it showcases how very clever he is. But this sort of response will entrap the superiority theorist in a dilemma. For if the laughter corresponds to Allen's recognition of his surpassing cleverness, the audience must be aware of their inferiority to Allen. Yet if the laughter correlates with the audience's feelings of superiority, why does Allen enjoy his own shtik?

Moreover, children laugh at an extremely early age at things such as funny faces and peekaboo games, but it is difficult to presume that they have yet evolved anything worth calling a concept of superiority, let alone a *self* to feel it. And, in any event, how would superiority figure in an account of laughter in response to a peekaboo game? When the caregiver reappears, who is supposed to be feeling superior? But then why does the child laugh?

Furthermore, we sometimes laugh at comic characters whose behaviour is decidedly superior to anything we could imagine achieving ourselves. For instance, in the film *Our Hospitality*, the character played by Buster Keaton is trapped on the ledge of a waterfall by a rope that has tethered him to an immovable log. At the same time, he sees that his beloved is about to be flung by the flowing waters over the cascade.

But, with lighting ingenuity, the Keaton character suddenly redeploys the rope that shackles him in order to swing to rescue, to catch his girlfriend as agilely as any trapeze artist might, and to swoop their way safely to the ground (see Figure 1). The audience bursts into laughter but its amusement is not based upon feeling superior to Keaton. Rather, we marvel while witnessing this astounding display of calculation and dexterity as Keaton reverses a dire situation into a triumphant one. His performance mixes an understanding of the physics of things with the athleticism of an Olympian gymnast in ways that very few can match, but still the audience as a whole is convulsed with the laughter of comic amusement. In such a case, it makes no sense to say that our laughter emanates from our feelings of superiority towards Keaton. If anything along this line of thought occurs to us, it is more likely that we realize that we are inferior to the Keaton character with respect to his remarkable combination of lightning thought and action. We should feel humility rather than arrogance.

Similarly, there are wordsmiths whose wit astonishes us as we cherish and repeat their sayings. Yet when Oscar Wilde advises

1. **Buster Keaton, _Our Hospitality_**

that 'One should be careful in one's choice of enemies' or observes that 'it is a terrible thing for a man to find out suddenly that all his life he has been speaking the truth,' or when Billy Wilder notes that 'Hindsight is twenty-twenty,' we do not swell up with sudden glory. If anything, we should feel humility in the face of their verbal ingenuity.

Here the superiority theorist may counter that listeners garner feelings of superiority by congratulating themselves that they are smart enough to appreciate the wordplay. But how can they avoid the realization that they are not as smart as those who created the word wit in the first place?

Superiority theorists may concoct increasingly ad hoc explanations to accommodate cases like these; however, as the explanations become more and more intricate, they become less and less convincing.

Frequently the source of comic amusement appears altogether irrelevant to issues of superiority and inferiority. Consider the cartoon of the medicine cabinet packed with apples (see Figure 2). Surely it is funny by way of being a clever visualization of the proverb 'An apple a day keeps the doctor away.' But to whom should we feel superior on encountering this visual witticism? Having fruit in your diet is a healthy regime; thus the cabinet owner is no fool. And the cartoonist is patently both visually and verbally deft—more talented in this respect than most of us who chuckle at his efforts. Consequently, it again appears that the capacity to elicit feelings of superiority is not a necessary feature of humour.

Nor is the recognition of our superiority to others a sufficient condition for laughter. As Francis Hutcheson pointed out in the 18th century, we realize that we are superior to oysters but we don't laugh at them. Nor, Hutcheson noted, do we

2. Cartoon by Robert Mankoff

laugh at heretics, although presumably the true believer should feel quite superior to them. Consequently, although the superiority theory appears to work well with many examples, at the same time there is a great deal of data which defies it.

The Hobbesian version of the superiority theory is framed in terms of laughter, and is putatively an account of the springs thereof. Undoubtedly, this enhances the intuitive plausibility of the theory, since, as may be readily observed, laughter often accompanies triumph. However, there remains the real question of whether laughter is, in fact, the proper object of analysis for a theory of humour.

For, on the one hand, laughter is a response not only to humour but also to tickling, nitrous oxide, belladonna, atropine, amphetamine, cannabis, alcohol, the gelastic seizures that accompany certain epileptic fits, nervousness, hebephrenia, not to mention sex, and, of course, victory. Indeed, the most effective elicitor of laughter is laughter, but bouts of contagious laughter need not be incited or sustained by guffaws in response to humour. On the other hand, some humour elicits not laughter but only a mild sensation of joy or lightness, i.e. levity. Thus, in focusing upon laughter, it is not clear that Hobbes's theory is really a theory of humour at all.

A theory of humour need be concerned only with amused laughter—the laughter that issues from comic amusement—and there is no reason to suppose that triumphant laughter, say, is amused laughter. To determine that would require an analysis of comic amusement. But it is doubtful that the superiority theory can provide an analysis of amusement, since the object of the passion that concerns Hobbes is the self triumphant, which does not seem to be the object of comic amusement, even if a sense of superiority can cause a certain type of laughter.

The incongruity theory

Many of the limitations of Hobbes's superiority theory were noted in the 18th century by Francis Hutcheson, who contributed to its replacement with what has come to be known as the *incongruity theory* of humour. In this view, the object of comic amusement is incongruity or, perhaps better, *perceived* incongruity.

Maybe the germ of this proposal was already present in the classical superiority theories of the ancients who thought the proper objects of comedy were people who are worse than average and therefore, perforce, deviations from the norm. However, this suggestion is too narrow since, as we have seen in cases like those of Keaton and Wilde, comedy may issue from excellence.

According to Hutcheson, the cause of laughter resides in contrasts such as between 'grandeur, dignity, sanctity and perfection and ideas of meanness, baseness, profanity...[This] seems to be the very spirit of burlesque; and the better part of raillery and jest is founded upon it.' Hutcheson's contemporary, James Beattie, concurred, generalizing beyond the contrasts named by Hutcheson and noting that 'laughter arises from the view of two or more inconsistent, unsuitable, or incongruous parts or circumstances, considered as united in complex object or assemblage, or as acquiring a sort of mutual relation from the peculiar manner in which the mind takes notice of them.' To date, as mentioned earlier, the incongruity theory of humour has attracted the largest allegiance among philosophers and psychologists.

According to the incongruity theory, what is key to comic amusement is a deviation from some presupposed norm—that is to say, an anomaly or an incongruity relative to some framework governing the ways in which we think the world is or should be. Sometimes this idea is stated in terms of a subversion of expectation. Yet this may be misleading. For often we are comically amused by outcomes we anticipate with mounting mirth—as in a slapstick comedy when the policeman, distracted by some passing beauty, walks into an open manhole.

Another reason to suspect that surprise is not necessary for comic amusement is that researchers have discovered that people derive more pleasure from jokes where they see the punchline coming—that is to say, from jokes where they are not surprised. This is probably one of the reasons why people like to repeat jokes and witticisms that they and their listeners already know. But, in any event, such phenomena indicate that surprise is not required for comic amusement.

Furthermore, when listening to a joke, we generally do not have any inkling—any *specific* expectations—about where it is headed. When the punchline is delivered, it is not as though it displaces some other specific thought that we had in mind. We are surprised, if the joke is effective—although as we've seen from our previous example of the slapstick policeman, our surprise is not necessary for comic amusement.

If we want to employ the language of *expectations* with respect to comic amusement, then we should not be thinking of specific expectations, such as 'How exactly will Pat in the opening joke respond to the bartender?' Rather, we should be thinking of our global expectations about how the world is or should be.

Incongruity is a comparative notion. It presupposes that something is discordant with something else. With respect to comic amusement, that *something else* is how the world is or should be.

Comic amusement emerges against a backdrop of presumed congruities or norms. Moreover, because we assume so many congruities or norms in order to wend our way through the world, there are an indeterminately large number of things that are potentially perceivable as incongruous.

Schopenhauer, for example, thought of the object of comic amusement along the lines of a category mistake or an absurdity, as in the case of Pat the Irishman, who understands the concept of 'being on the wagon' to be consistent with downing two drinks for his brothers, so long as he refrains from tossing one back for himself. The oxymoron 'If pigs could fly...' is funny because it misplaces swine in the category of things that can fly. Likewise the

American comedienne Sarah Silverman is comically effective because it is so incongruous that such a sweet-looking young woman spouts such obscenities and vitriol; she appears stereotypically 'innocent' but then speaks in a way that would make a sailor blush.

The leading idea of the incongruity theory is that comic amusement comes with the apprehension of incongruity. We are amused by the animated fowl in the film *Chicken Run* because their movements, their behaviour, and their very look call to mind human beings. However, this is incongruous or absurd. It would be a category mistake to subsume chickens under the concept of human being: it would violate a standing concept; it would be an incongruous instantiation of the kind in question. The makers of *Chicken Run*, nevertheless, invite us to contemplate just such a prospect, and in doing so they elicit comic amusement.

Schopenhauer's theory of humour, like Kierkegaard's, parses 'incongruity' in terms of contradiction. That is why we are amused when we hear Yogi Berra observe of a restaurant that 'No one goes there any more because it is too crowded' or Michael Curtiz say 'Include me out.' Because they violate and disrupt norms, violations of logic, deductive and inductive, formal and informal, they are incongruities and, therefore, staples of comedy.

Likewise, we find 'Due to the recession, my sister has received a number of pre-declined credit cards in the mail' funny because the notion of a pre-declined credit card offer strikes us as self-contradictory, while the joke in which the overweight customer asks to have his pizza sliced into four pieces rather than eight because he's on a diet is an outright logical howler.

But we abide by many other laws than those of logic and the grammar of concepts; consequently, the ambit of humour is much broader than Schopenhauer's very tidy theory suggests. In addition to violations of logic, tampering with natural laws can also invite comic amusement. Part of the pervasive charm of the Harry Potter series is the way in which it splices together elements of the Muggle world, with its physics, and the wizard world, with its magic, in delightful inventions, including flying cars, invisible railroad platforms, and immaterial buses. The humour here resides in the fact that, given magic, it seems strange that the wizard world would retain any vestiges of Muggle mechanics, especially when these inventions malfunction, despite the intervention of sorcery.

In *Harry Potter and the Chamber of Secrets*, incongruity erupts when it is said that when the mandrakes get over their acne, they'll be ready for action, thereby perpetrating a category error that yokes together the disparate species of the human and the vegetable. Similarly, the very idea of SpongeBob SquarePants—a talking soap pad—is incongruous.

Moreover, not only beings but also machines can be improbably incongruous, as when the American stand-up comedienne Chelsea Handler imagines what she would consider the ideal gift—a vibrator that also makes tacos.

Biological anomalies can also serve as a provenance for comic amusement. One example of this might be thought of as developmental incongruities. For instance, there is a room in the Frick Museum in New York where panels by François Boucher show very young children at work in very adult roles (the panel *The Arts and the Sciences: Chemistry* shows a veritable infant at his cauldron cooking up some formula). The joke here is the incongruous mismatch between the child and the adult occupation.

Nor is this variety of humour a thing of the past. Currently on American TV, there is a commercial encouraging personal stock trading that presents us with an infant—whose mouth has been digitally jigsawed to form adult words—recommending that the process is so easy a child can do it. Likewise, in the motion picture

Step Brothers, the characters played by Will Farrell and John C. Reilly are adult men in their forties who behave as though they were twelve years old.

In addition to the laws of logic and nature, we operate in accordance with norms of morality, prudence, and etiquette. Hence, it is unsurprising that much humour involves immorality, reckless and extravagant behaviour, and gaucherie. Using a person as an armrest, as Charlie Chaplin sometimes does, or a tablecloth as an handkerchief, are both incongruous, since they represent deviations from normatively governed behaviour. The former example violates morality—treating, as Chaplin does, a person as merely a means—while the latter is ill mannered.

Among the conventional rules we live by are not only those of politeness but also those of language, including not just grammar but conversational maxims. For example, conversational protocols are violated when in answer to the question 'Do you know what time it is?' one replies by simply saying 'Yes.'

A central conversational maxim enjoins us to avoid ambiguity. However, as is obvious, a major source of humour, the pun, flouts that directive as a very condition of its existence. A pun can incite levity by shifting the likely meaning of a word or phrase in a specific context to a secondary or metaphorical meaning. Or it may exchange the predictable usage of a word for that of one of its homonyms, as in: 'Why did the moron stay up all night? He was studying for his blood test.' That is, a pun is incongruous because it involves activating word meanings that are out of place, given the direction of the surrounding discourse. Groucho Marx's puns frequently derail, in a single blow, the rules of semantics, syntax, and conversation.

Puns may also be incongruous by being utter nonsense. I am told that there is a pancake house in New Brunswick, New Jersey, called Hansel and Griddle. This makes no sense, although it sounds close to sense—or to something recognizable, at least—because it sounds so much like the names of the characters in a famous fairy tale. Here the incongruity involves the interplay of sense and nonsense, as Sigmund Freud discusses with respect to what he calls innocent jokes.

Moreover, the wacky logical inferences so frequently indulged by the denizens of jokes, satires, and burlesques also count as incongruities; they are absurdities, given the laws of logic, again, both deductive and inductive, formal and informal. Irony too can serve up comic humour, because it traffics in contradiction, saying one thing while meaning its opposite. Word wit may also function by taking a cliché or well-known verbal formula and reversing its meaning, as Voltaire did when he observed, 'Despite the ministrations of the greatest doctors in Europe, the patient survived.' Speaking very broadly, norms of appropriateness govern almost every aspect of our lives, opening up, thereby, the possibility of humour with respect to sexual behaviour, cleanliness, attire, and much else. We presuppose norms of human intelligence and physical condition. Hence, it is no accident that so many clowns are inhumanly stupid and exceedingly fat or skinny.

Roughly, the notion of incongruity presupposed by the incongruity theory can initially be described as a problematization of sense. This can occur when concepts or rules are violated or transgressed. But the scope of these transgressions need not be limited to conceptual mistakes, linguistic improprieties, or logical errors. Sense can also be problematized by being stretched to the breaking point.

Thus, it is very common to field comic teams composed of a very thin man and a very fat man (e.g. Don Quixote and Sancho Panza, Laurel and Hardy, Abbott and Costello). In this case, there is no category error. However, we are presented with instantiations of the concept of the human being that lie at the extreme ends of the relevant category: the characters are so dissimilar that one is, oddly enough, struck by the heterogeneity of the category, rather than by its homogeneity.

Similarly, incongruity accrues when a concept is instantiated in a highly unlikely way rather than in an outright erroneous way. Shown a ninety-eight-pound weakling outfitted in the gear of a sumo wrestler, we are struck by the incongruity since the character is such an unrepresentative example of our stereotype for athletes of this sort.

As the preceding example indicates, not only can concepts be problematized for the purpose of incongruity, but so can stereotypes. Our stereotypes can be distorted either through the exaggeration of stereotypical features or through their diminution. Caricature often exaggerates—as in cartoons of the actor Edward G. Robinson that enlarged his lips enormously or the many images of FDR with his cigarette holder clenched in his mouth at a pronounced angle. Indeed, exaggeration is a standard strategy throughout burlesque, parody, and satire. The previous example of the skinny sumo wrestler, on the other hand, is an example of incongruous diminution.

Stereotypes may also be exploited for the purpose of amusement by uniting comic couples with opposing character traits: Don Quixote's idealism and Sancho Panza's practical cunning; Bertie Wooster's empty-headedness and Jeeves's near omniscience; Dr Bone's obsessiveness and Susan's hysteria in the movie *Bringing Up Baby*. But reversing stereotypes also works comically, as in George Herriman's comic strip *Krazy Kat*, where a mouse attacks a dog, or in Dr Seuss's *Horton Hears a Who!*, where an elephant is pushed around by lesser creatures including monkeys and a kangaroo.

Similarly, lecherous clerics have been comic regulars at least since the Renaissance, since their behaviour is so at odds with our concept of their station. The abbess in *The Decameron* who accidentally doffs an undergarment instead of her wimple is doubly anomalous both in terms of her anomalous headgear as well as what it implies about her relation to her vow of chastity.

Rowan Atkinson, as quoted by Susan Stewart, is speaking as an incongruity theorist when he defines humour as behaving in an unusual way, being in an unusual place, or being the wrong size, as in the case of our diminutive sumo wrestler. For an example of unusual behaviour, recall the scene in which Gussie Fink-Nottle delivers a drunken oration at the awards ceremony featured in P.G. Wodehouse's *Right Ho Jeeves*. The episode is uproarious exactly because Gussie's impolite ramblings so ill befit the decorum expected of speakers on such occasions. When portly men like Fatty Arbuckle and Benny Hill dress up in women's clothing, they are, in the eyes of their culture, behaving unusually, as were Ernie Kovacs's televisual terpsichores when they performed *Swan Lake* in gorilla costumes.

Conflicting viewpoints supply another source of incongruity. In comic narratives—including novels, plays, and films—it frequently happens that certain characters misperceive their circumstances; they may think they are speaking to a gardener when in fact they are speaking to the master of the house. The audience is aware of this and tracks the spectacle under two alternative, but nevertheless conflicting, interpretations: the limited perspective of the mistaken character and the omniscient perspective of the narrator. Inasmuch as these viewpoints effectively contradict each other, the incongruity theorist counts them as further instances of incongruous juxtaposition.

Some jokes are called meta-jokes because they call attention to the conventions of joke telling by deviating from them. The joke—'Why did the chicken cross the road? To get to the other side'—is a meta-joke, because it violates, while also revealing, our conventional or normative expectations about jokes, namely that they possess surprising (and faux informative) punchlines. That chickens cross roads to get to the other side is hardly informative; being told that they do so is anomalous only as the conclusion of a joke. Likewise, non sequiturs are incongruous, because they subvert our expectations that conversations and stories will be comprised of parts that are coherently and proportionately linked.

Some jokes accrue added enjoyment for incongruously reversing comic stereotypes. For example, in this joke, the dumb blonde outsmarts the cunning lawyer:

On a flight from London to Chicago, a beautiful blonde takes her seat next to a man in a grey sharkskin suit who turns out to be a lawyer.

The lawyer looks her over and says, 'Let's play a game.'

'What game?' asks the blonde.

'I ask you a question. If you can't answer it, you give me five pounds. You ask me a question. If I can't answer it, I give you fifty pounds.'

The blonde agrees and the lawyer goes first.

'What is *habeas corpus*?' The blonde quietly hands him five pounds.

Then it's the blonde's turn: 'What is grey and purple and chartreuse when it goes up the hill with three legs, and blue, red, and white when it comes down the hill on one leg?'

'I don't know,' says the lawyer, handing her fifty pounds. Then he takes his turn: 'So what is it?'

The blonde hands him five pounds.

So what starts as a dumb blonde/smart lawyer joke becomes a dumb lawyer/smart blonde joke.

Emotional incoherence can also figure as incongruity, as when a character matches the wrong feeling or attitude with a situation, or simply vastly exaggerates an apposite one, as Jackie Gleason frequently did while playing Ralph in the American sitcom *The Honeymooners*, exploding, as he often did at least once per episode, at decibel levels far above the norm. Similarly, Larry David, in the

American TV series *Curb Your Enthusiasm*, worries life's small anomalies into major confrontations and/or embarrassments when interacting with other characters. He lacks impulse control altogether; he does not know when to end a conversation or to cease pressing a point. His enthusiasm is utterly inappropriate, while also un-curbable. Larry David's genius, as TV critic Gillian Flynn observes, involves 'taking little annoyances, indignities, and offenses and worrying them until they bubble into fantastically overblown debacles.'

Of course, emotional incongruity may not only obtain when the emotional volume is perceived to be too much; too little affect in certain situations is equally risible, as in the anecdote of the lady and the obituary:

> Julie calls the newspaper to post a notice of the death of her husband Fred. She asks the clerk at the paper how much this will cost.
> The clerk replies, 'Five pounds a word.'
> 'Oh my,' Julie sighs resignedly. 'Well, write this: Fred died.'
> After Julie hangs up, the clerk feels badly about the widow Julie's plight.
> He calls back and, lying, says: 'I forgot to tell you that for every two words you pay for in an obituary this week, you get three more words for free.'
> 'Wonderful,' Julie exclaims. 'Write this: Fred died; Jaguar for sale.'

There are also standards of grace and taste, which when violated by pronounced clumsiness and vulgarity can provoke comic amusement. Slapstick comedy, of course, depends on the former; obscene jokes and bathroom humour on the latter. Rabelais strikes a comic chord, for example, when all the dogs in the vicinity drench the Parisian lady as if, to speak anachronistically, she were a lamp post, and also when Panurge so confounds the English theologian in their disputation, which is conducted in improvised sign language, that the British cleric collapses and soils himself. Since sex and sexual behaviour are freighted with so many norms and stereotypes, they too are a natural breeding ground for humour. It is because of our gender stereotypes regarding manliness that we find it so hilariously funny that Wodehouse's Roderick Spode, a fascist bully, is secretly a passionate designer of women's lingerie.

Likewise we know the decorum that is supposed to be maintained when dealing with religious topics, which makes religious topics ripe for comic amusement—as when on *The Sarah Silverman Program*, the eponymous comic makes love to God, who turns out to be a black man who, in addition, she dumps.

Comic amusement, according to the incongruity theory, presupposes that the audience has a working knowledge of all the congruities—concepts, rules, expectations—that the humour in question disturbs or violates; and perhaps part of the pleasure of humour involves exercising our ability to access this background information, often very rapidly.

Prototypical incongruities, then, include deviations, disturbances, or problematizations of our concepts, rules, laws of logic and reasoning, stereotypes, norms of morality, of prudence, and of etiquette, contradictory points of view presented in tandem, and, in general, subversions of our commonplace expectations, including our expectations concerning standard emotional scenarios and schemas, our norms of grace, taste, and even the very forms of comedy itself. Given this list of prototypical incongruities, the theorist can begin to chart a theory of humour.

Humour, for the incongruity theory, is a response-dependent property of a certain type of stimulus, viz. stimuli that support our amusement in response to their display of the property of incongruity (or incongruous properties). That is, perceived incongruity is the primary object of the mental state of comic amusement; one is in a state of comic amusement only if the object of that state is a perceived incongruity. This state may be in response to *found* humour; we may suddenly notice that something encountered in everyday life is in some way funny (incongruous)—a Smart car parked next to a stretched Hummer, perhaps. Or we may come across an accidental absurdity when reading the mangled English of a menu in a foreign country, such as the advertisement for a dinner special that offers: 'Turkey €2.25; Chicken or Beef, €2.35; Children €2.00.' Of course, comic amusement may also take hold in response to *invented* humour, such as jokes, which are intended to bring incongruities to our attention, usually forcefully.

This suggestion is an advance on the superiority theory, since perceived incongruity, or absurdity, would appear to be a more likely object of comic amusement than the self (which is what the superiority theorist seems to suggest by making laughter an expression of pride). After all, feelings of superiority and accompanying squeals of cruel laughter can attend something that has nothing funny about it, such as the bloody slaying of a sworn enemy. In contrast, the derailment of sense is a natural candidate for comic laughter, whether at our own expense, at the expense of others, or at no one's expense; for example, we may be comically amused when we find a plucked chicken in our running bag or a frozen turkey in the washing machine in the launderette because those are absurd places for them to be, even if we are not laughing at someone else, real or imagined.

However, perceived incongruity is at best no more than a necessary condition for comic amusement. That is, incongruity alone is not enough to make something funny. As Alexander Bain, the 19th-century philosopher, psychologist, and educationalist, pointed out, incongruity is a very baggy concept; it is too loose to perform the work that the incongruity theorists want it to do. Bain argued that incongruity could not possibly supply a sufficient condition for comic amusement, since there are many incongruities that engender other sorts of feelings. Indeed, there are many instances when we encounter incongruities that are hardly amusing.

Most patently, many incongruities are just as likely, or even more likely, to stir up fear and anxiety. Bela Lugosi, done up in his Dracula outfit, may cheer us in *Abbott and Costello Meet Frankenstein*, but in other contexts he is more apt to disturb. So even if incongruity is part of the story of comic amusement, it cannot be the whole story: incongruity simply does not correlate perfectly with comic amusement.

Often confrontations with incongruity and deviations from expectations are threatening occasions, fraught with anxiety. As psychologists have pointed out, if a total stranger makes funny faces at a small child, the child is apt to be frightened; but equally, if a familiar caregiver assumes the same funny (incongruous) face, the child is likely to giggle. What this indicates is that, in order for comic amusement to obtain, the percipient must feel unthreatened by it. They must regard the incongruity not as a source of anxiety but rather as an opportunity to relish its absurdity.

Cases of found humour, then, require that the situations that comically amuse us not be ones in which we feel personal threat. We will not be amused if the galumphing three-hundred-pound footballer is headed on a lethal collision course towards us; nor will we be comically amused if we perceive the situation as in some other way dangerous, for example as threatening harm to others; for that will produce anxiety.

Likewise, with respect to invented humour, Aristotle notes that comedy should not involve pain or destruction, or, perhaps more accurately, it should not draw focused attention upon suffering. It should be kept off stage, so to speak. Thus, one factor that needs to be added to perceived incongruity in order for the incongruity theory to approach adequacy is the recognition that for comic amusement to take off, it must occur in a context from which fear for ourselves and those we care about—including fictional characters—has been banished. Comic incongruities, in other words, must be non-threatening, or, at least, what is potentially threatening, frightening, or anxiety producing about them must be deflected and/or marginalized.

When someone is killed in a joke—as so many lawyers are—we are not treated to the gruesome details of their demise. Thus, when the lawyer in the outhouse in *Jurassic Park* is stomped to death by the T. Rex, the audience howls with glee. Had they been treated to a view of his broken body, accompanied by sobs of pain, their laughter would probably have been silenced. Similarly, jokesters do not dwell upon the agonies of the casualties in their stories. Moreover, the victims are generally people we don't care about and maybe even people we are encouraged to dislike—and even to imagine to be deserving of whatever they get (think of the lawyers again as they inhabit the unflagging lawyer jokes that circulate in the USA relentlessly).

Of course, those whom we care about can come in for a pummelling in humour, such as figures of slapstick like the Three Stooges, but it is significant that these figures are usually clowns, beings, that is, who are not quite human—creatures who can take a hit on the head with a sledgehammer and who then, after a brief swoon, are back in the game almost immediately.

Henri Bergson referred to this tolerance for comic brutality by means of the memorable phrase 'the momentary anaesthesia of the heart.' Yet I don't think that this should be understood to mean that comic amusement is altogether alien to emotion, but only that certain emotions—such as sympathy—are disengaged either by distracting our attention away from that which might enlist our sympathies for the characters in question, or by de-emphasizing the apparent degree of danger and/or pain that threatens them, or by portraying them as antipathetic, or by portraying them as other-than-normal humans, such as clowns and, therefore, not subject to the injuries to which flesh is heir.

Invented humour deploys various external and internal conventions in order to assure that its incongruities will not be anxiety producing. With respect to external factors, the anaesthesia of sympathy is secured insofar as the pertinent incongruity is generally introduced as non-threatening by conventional signals—such as the locution 'Did you hear the one about such and such?' and/or by changes in intonation—which herald a joking situation, which type of situation, in turn, is marked by custom as an arena for playfulness.

That is, these devices alert us to the proposition that now is the time to adopt comic distance. Characters, in other words, are about to be beaten, blown apart, defenestrated, and so on, but we should not worry about them. In short, these framing devices tell us that the imaginary beings in jokes and other comic forms are not quite like us ontologically and, therefore, what happens to them should not be a matter of our concern.

These conventional markers not only announce that the audience should not feel threatened themselves, but also mandate comic distance—an absence of empathy and moral concern for the characters in jokes and satires—which relieves us of worries and anxieties about what is happening to the beings that inhabit the joke worlds and other fictional environments of invented humour. They can be burning in hell or being eaten by sharks or falling from tall buildings, yet the external conventions that erect comic distance tell us to bracket any anxieties on their account.

Of course, not all humour comes labelled as such. Deadpan witticisms uttered 'in all seriousness' in the middle of a business meeting may not be externally packaged as something intended to be funny, but factors such as the extreme incongruity of the remark in its conversational context do the work here by first taking us aback and then disposing us, upon reflection, to realize its flagrant absurdity. Thus, where the remark is sadistic, the incongruity deflects our sympathy for its target and erects a wall of comic distance.

Furthermore, this comic distance or comic anaesthesia is not merely a function of conventions external to the humour in question. Jokes, slapstick, and the like, as already noted, are also internally structured in a way that supports bracketing anxiety by refraining from dwelling upon or calling attention to the consequences—physical, moral, or psychological—of the misfortunes that befall comic characters. That is, after we are told in a joke that some character is being eaten, we are not reminded that he would be bleeding profusely or that his family is now destitute, for that might elicit sympathy. In fact, invented humour generally trades in fictional worlds that are devoid of sustained acknowledgements of pain in such a way that our normal empathetic and moral responses remain in abeyance, thereby divesting the situation of the potential to provoke anxiety.

One apparent counter example to my conjecture that humorous incongruities are divested of elements that would recruit our anxieties for the victims of comic mayhem may appear to be many instances of black humour, such as dead baby jokes. These jokes certainly involve incongruities, if anything does, revelling as they do in the torture and/or death of infants. Consider: 'What is brown and gurgles? A baby casserole.' Who can deny that such treatment of innocents is the epitome of viciousness?

But these jokes apparently amuse many. At least two factors seem to come into play here. First, like all jokes, these specimens are framed as jokes, thereby invoking comic distance. But second, and perhaps more importantly, the babies are not really the butt of these jokes. The butt of dead baby jokes, and of black humour in general, are those sanctimonious folks whom we imagine will be outraged by the joke. Similarly, when we laugh in response to the cognitively challenged street person who smashes their head with bricks in *Monty Python*, our amusement, it seems to me, is not directed at them but at those people who have a tendency to sentimentalize mental deficiencies.

There is an episode of *South Park*, the American cartoon series, entitled 'Stanley's Cup,' in which, through a sequence of complicated events, the Pee-Wee hockey team, coached by the character Stan Marsh, winds up playing an adult, professional hockey team. The professionals, however, make no allowance for the youth and lack of experience and talent of the grade-schoolers and treat them as they would an adult team, including indulging in all the nastiness for which hockey pros are renowned. By the end of the episode, all the children are lying about, scattered, battered, and bloody on the ice.

But it is clear that the target of this black humour is not the children. Rather the episode is a parody of all of those syrupy exercises in underdog-ism in which the Bad News Bears (etc.) come from behind against the odds to save the day. 'Stanley's Cup' even has a boy with cancer who has asked the kids to win the game for him; he lives just long enough to learn his team has been creamed and then dies. Yet neither is he the target of the jibe here. Rather, it is all those sentimentalists who enjoy getting choked up at these wish-fulfilment fantasies. The creators of *South Park* just love to scandalize such folks. 'Stanley's Cup' is an animated dead baby joke.

In general, verbal jokes are on a continuum with practical jokes. There is an element of trickery about them. The jokester, that is, tricks the listener of the joke into finding the absurd conclusion of the joke to be somehow compellingly intelligible, when it is not. Perhaps the grain of truth in the superiority theory is that humour frequently has a butt, although, since often, as in the case of a joke, the butt is us, we cannot be laughing out of a sense of superiority. However, with respect to black humour, the trick is not being played upon the actual appreciator but upon the uptight audience whom we envision becoming apoplectically indignant when hearing such a joke, or, as in the case of 'Stanley's Cup,' seeing it played out.

André Breton, who came up with the notion of black humour, notes that such humour 'is the mortal enemy of sentimentality.' That is why the character played by Gaston Modot in Luis Buñuel's *l'Age d'Or*, steps on a bug wantonly, terrifies a little dog, cuffs an elderly lady, and mistreats a blind man. Black humour is a satire on conventional pieties. It is another way of outraging the bourgeoisie. Or, as a friend of mine, Joan Acocella, likes to say, 'It's a way of driving your mother insane.'

Parallel to the demand that the pertinent incongruities be unthreatening is a related requirement: that they not be annoying. Imagine the cutlery laid out for a formal dinner. Suppose that the salad fork is in the wrong place. If you are the sort of person who is disturbed by such deviations from the norm, you will not be capable of finding this amusing. On the other hand, if you are more easy-going about such matters and also aware of the incongruity, it may elicit a chuckle. That is, you may find the error amusing or not. But if you find it genuinely amusing, you cannot find it annoying. Moreover, if you find black humour amusing, you can be sure that there are others who will find it annoying, even extremely so. And you revel in their discomfort.

Comic amusement for the incongruity theory, then, requires as its object a perceived incongruity, of the sort inventoried above, which is neither threatening nor anxiety producing nor annoying but which can, on the contrary, be enjoyed. Invented humour is that which is intended to afford such a state. But, of course, this is not yet an adequate definition of comic amusement, since the definition so far could be satisfied by mathematical puzzles whose solutions, though sometimes occasioning laughter, are not prima facie either humorous or appropriate objects of comic amusement. Indeed, we take pleasure in mastering all sorts of puzzles and anomalies, both practical and theoretical, but do not consider that a pretext for laughter.

The problem here is that our responses to incongruities are not partitioned just into being threatened and/or annoyed as opposed to being comically amused. Often incongruities simply puzzle us and motivate us to solve the problem at hand. So what is the difference between things such as mathematical theorems and puzzles that challenge us to enjoy resolving them versus humour?

Of course, at this point it may strike some of you as rather feckless to attempt to distinguish sharply between the pleasures experienced when confronting puzzles and problems, on the one hand, and the comic amusement that results from humour, on the other, since a large portion of comic amusement is inspired by jokes—whether of the riddle variety or the narrative kind—and those jokes typically involve puzzles, a.k.a. as punchlines, whose anomalousness gives birth to interpretations that are outwardly designed to dispel their incongruity. However, the interpretation the punchline propones is categorically different from the thinking that we typically employ when attempting to solve puzzles and problems.

In order to see what I am getting at, consider this joke:

> The lone survivor of an airplane crash is marooned on a deserted island in the middle of the Pacific Ocean. After many years, he is rescued by a passing ocean liner. The doctor who examines him says, 'You're in great health, but tell me one thing. Why did you build two synagogues on the island?' The survivor answers: 'The one on the north side of the island is my synagogue. The other one I wouldn't step into.'

Here the punchline explains the puzzle of why there are two synagogues on an island with one inhabitant, but it does so at the cost of compounding the absurdity. For the joke invites us to imagine—against anything the interpretive principle of charity would recommend—a man so improbable that he would build a structure for the sole purpose of not entering it. In this joke, an answer is supplied to the puzzle, yet the answer itself is an absurdity or an incongruity, equal to the first one, which does not prompt further interrogation but which simply jollies us.

In contrast, when we are engaged in *authentic* puzzle solving, our pleasures blossom once we achieve our commitment to really resolving the pertinent incongruities—that is, to making genuine sense and dispelling apparent nonsense. In the state of comic amusement, on the other hand, we are not concerned to discover legitimate resolutions to incongruities, but at best, as in the case of jokes, to marvel at the appearance of sense, or the appearance of congruity, in what is otherwise recognized as palpable nonsense. With puzzle solving, properly so-called, our enjoyment depends on finding or trying to find an actual answer to our question—one that accords congruously with how the world is or should be. On the other hand, with respect to jokes and the like, one puzzle or incongruity gives way to another, and we leave it at that. The result of a joke is a derangement of sense. But when we engage in genuine puzzle solving—from crossword puzzles to mathematical theorems—we aim at discovering the right answers and take pleasure in that, whereas with things such as jokes, we are happy—really happy—with the wrong answers.

Moreover, with invented humour, that we are to suspend our inclinations to puzzle solving is signalled by the external conventions and internal structures of the pertinent genres. That is, the conventions that indicate the presence of invented humour announce that genuine resolutions of incongruity are not in the offing, while at the same time the content of the humour defies veridical resolution. Whereas, in problem solving, enjoyment with respect to the puzzle, our enjoyment attaches first and foremost to finding an authentic solution, with comic amusement the pleasure focuses upon the incongruity itself.

Summarizing *provisionally* one version of the incongruity theory, then, someone is comically amused if and only if (i) the object of their mental state is a perceived incongruity, which (ii) they regard as neither threatening or anxiety producing nor (iii) annoying and which (iv) they do not approach with a genuine, puzzle-solving attitude, but which, rather, (v) they enjoy precisely for their perception of its incongruity. Humour is the response-dependent property that affords comic amusement. Found humour differs from invented humour in that the latter is proffered with the intention, supported by external and internal features of the presentation, to afford comic amusement, whereas in the case of found humour the percipient themselves not only discovers the incongruities but brackets wariness, annoyance, and the disposition towards puzzle solving on their own, thereby opening themselves to the possibility of enjoying the stimulus.

However appealing the incongruity theory of humour may appear, it does have at least one problem that cannot be overlooked: it is the very notion of incongruity. For we do not have an absolutely clear definition of it. In the past, when philosophers such as Schopenhauer attempted to define humour rigorously—he thought it was essentially a category mistake—the definition has appeared to be too narrow to accommodate everything we would typically count as humorous. This then tempts one to try to elucidate incongruity, as above, by enumerating prototypical examples. Yet these examples run a very broad gamut of cases, ranging from conceptual and logical errors to inappropriate table manners to offishness to subverted norms in general. Thus one fears that such an imprecise notion of incongruity may not be exclusive enough, especially if it unqualifiedly countenances something as pervasive as the subversion of our global expectations as an incongruity. So an important question about the incongruity theory is whether it can be tightened beyond what has been offered so far—a question to which we shall return after reviewing three more competing theories of humour.

The release theory

The third traditional theory of humour is called the *release theory*. Some commentators have speculated that Aristotle may have propounded such a theory in the lost, second book of his *Poetics*, which we are told analysed comedy. Since the first book explicated tragedy in terms of the notion of catharsis, which some commentators interpret as purgation of accumulated emotions of pity and fear, it has been hypothesized that it is probable Aristotle would have similarly regarded comedy as a way of dissipating built-up feelings.

The Earl of Shaftesbury suggested that comedy released our otherwise constrained, natural free spirits, a kind of view shared by Freud, who argued that jokes liberate the energy expended by rationality to repress both infantile nonsense and tendentious feelings. Similarly, Herbert Spencer regarded laughter as a discharge of nervous energy which occurs when the mind, taken unawares, is led from the consciousness of something large (grave or at least serious) to something small (silly or trivial). Presumably, when this happens, the nervous energy stored up to grapple with serious matters is displaced or vented into laughter, and thereby flushed out of the system.

The theories of Spencer and Freud have the liability of presupposing hydraulic views of the mind which are highly dubious. Both postulate the existence of mental energy that behaves like water—flowing in certain channels, circumventing blockages, and seeking outlets as the pressure builds. Their language, though couched in the scientific jargon of their day, seems at best metaphorical from the viewpoint of the present. Or, to put the objection in a less ad hominem form, their theories assume that there is something to be released, something that is gathering and/or has been repressed, and that this is some quantity of energy. But there seem to be scant scientific grounds for such assumptions.

It might seem that the release theory could be rephrased in less contentious language, perhaps using some notion of expectations. When we are asked a riddle or told a joke, it might be said, naturally enough, that expectation builds as we await the punchline. We are curious about how this comic discourse will end. When the punchline arrives, the pressure of those expectations is released and laughter ensues.

Perhaps this is what Kant had in mind when he maintained that 'Laughter is an affection arising from sudden transformation of a strained expectation into nothing.' That is, our curiosity glues us to the joke (or the joke holds us in its grip), but when the joke concludes with an absurd punchline (Kant's 'nothing'), the hold of the joke upon the listener loosens.

But it does not seem that the notion of release provides a necessary, accurate, or even a desirable way of describing how expectations are engaged by jokes.

Jokes and riddles ideally inspire a desire for closure in listeners—a desire, for example, to hear the answer to the riddle or the punchline of the joke. When the answer or punchline arrives, that desire is satisfied, and such satisfaction contributes to the enjoyment that follows—enjoyment that is often marked by laughter. But there is no cause to speak of release here; talk of expectations or desires and their fulfilment suffices.

Maybe it will be proposed that, once our desires are fulfilled, we are in effect released from them. But since they are *our* desires, this seems an unproductively metaphorical way of speaking. It says no more than that we no longer have the desire in question, because it has been satisfied. After all, we possess the desire; the desire does not possess us. Just as it makes more sense to say—from a non-theological point of view—that when we die we are no longer alive (rather than that we have been released from life), so it is better to say we no longer have the expectations, instead of that we have been released from them, when those expectations have been satisfied.

Jokes belong to the category of what might be called temporal humour; they promise closure. But not all humour is like this. Some humour involves no working-up of expectations. So even if we accepted the release theory as an account of the play of expectation in temporal forms of humour, such as jokes, it could not be extended to forms of humour that do not build up expectations over time. When the ninety-eight-pound sumo wrestler appears on stage, or when we find a turkey in the washing machine, we are comically amused. But it is wrong to say that our expectations have had anything done to them, since in these cases we had no specific antecedent expectations collecting in our consciousness.

Here, of course, it is open to the proponent of the release theory to attempt to postulate that there is always some subconscious processing, however brief, going on, and that this involves expectations. But until one is told more about the way in which these alleged processes work, this gambit sounds exceedingly ad hoc.

Alternatively, it may be said that we do have the requisite expectations without hypothesizing subconscious processing, i.e. we have standing expectations about what is normal, and it is these expectations that have been subverted. Thus we are released from our standing or normal expectations. And, it might be added, this is also what happens when we are confronted with the nonsensical endings of jokes, as well as with confrontations with ninety-eight-pound sumo wrestlers and turkeys in washing machines. But again, the idea that we are possessed by and then released from our normal conceptual schemes seems a strained way of speaking, unless we suppose that those expectations are invested with powers to constrain or to repress, or that they require some supplemental quotient of mental pressure in order to continue functioning.

Yet that then sends us back to our earlier problem—the tendency of release theories to proliferate unwarranted mental entities and/or processes. Nor does it seem plausible to imagine that having our normal expectations about the world is like being shackled by them, since, in this instance, the 'shackles' are us.

Of course, it may be possible to frame something like a release theory without committing oneself to any exotic mental phenomena. It has already been suggested that when presented with an anomaly—such as the punchline of a joke—one is affronted with a challenge, an incongruity which may be appraised as threatening, annoying, in need of a solution, or amusing. That is, the punchline is a difficulty to be negotiated; when we reckon that it is simply amusing, the difficulty is removed. From being primed for effort, a sense of effortlessness, ease, and relaxation ensues. An initial intuition that something is being demanded of us disappears, resulting in relief.

Probably the disappearance of that momentary intimation of the need to mobilize our resources, especially our cognitive resources, is what Kant meant by 'nothing.' However, I think a better way to label the relevant transition might be to talk in terms of a mental experience of being unburdened cognitively—an experience, that is, imbued with a quality of sudden lightness or lightening (as in 'lightening a load') which we may call *levity*.

Nevertheless, even if all comic amusement is marked by such levity, a release theory along these lines would still fall short of a satisfactory definition of comic amusement. For this interval of suddenly being unburdened, phenomenologically speaking, accompanies many experiences other than comic amusement. Similar experiences attend the moment when one deftly evades what seems to be an all-but-inevitable checkmate. Thus, a release theory even of the sort now under consideration would at best only give us a necessary condition for comic amusement. To get a

41

sharper account of humour, as we shall see, may require marrying this notion of relief or relaxation with some other features—perhaps features already identified by a previous theory.

The play theory

The notion that humour involves playful relaxation, which serves as the basis of the *play theory* of comic amusement, can be found in Aristotle's remarks about such play as a complement to the life of activity. This theme is taken up by St Thomas Aquinas, who in his *Summa Theologica* recommends play as a remedy for the weariness of the active life, especially the active mental life. He writes: 'Those words and deeds in which nothing is sought beyond the soul's pleasure are called pleasure and humorous, and it is necessary to make use of them at times for solace of soul.' Arguably, the play theory is a kind of release theory—comic amusement as a release from the burdens of everyday activity, and, if you are a theologian, from philosophical activity, which is even more arduous. Max Eastman, in the 20th century, defended such a view, assimilating humour as a kind of play.

And surely there is a strikingly recurring pattern of association between humour and play. Much, if not most, humour is indulged in moments of relaxation and leisure, indeed, riffing or joshing with one's friends, family, and associates is itself a form of relaxation. And it certainly also makes sense to refer to a great deal of humour in terms of play—playing with words or word play, playing with ideas, and so forth. Much humour, in short, coincides with play or playing. But it is not clear that humour and playing are identical.

For even if play or playing were a necessary condition for humour, they would not be sufficient, since there are so many other forms of play that do not involve humour. Draughts is a form of play, but it has nothing essential to do with comic amusement. And so on for an indeterminately large number of leisure activities whose enumeration I leave up to the reader.

But, on the other hand, it is not clear that play is even a necessary condition for humour. The problem here is our concept of play. How are we to define it? One temptation is to stipulate that play is disengaged from life—that it is not serious. But if that is what is meant by *play* then humour is not necessarily play, since a major form of humour is satire—both of society at large and of features of our conspecifics such as hypocrisy. Humour need not be divorced from life. Consequently, if play is defined as disengaged from life or as non-serious, humour does not fit squarely in the genus of play, since some (much) humour, like satire, is engaged and serious.

In order for some version of the play theory of comic amusement to succeed we would need a better idea of what kind of play is germane to humour. Perhaps elements of the play theory can be incorporated in broader theories of comic amusement along with elements of some of the other theories of humour. Surely the idea that comic amusement has some connection with play is highly plausible, given the frequent correlation of the two. But what that connection or those connections might be remains to be excavated.

The dispositional theory

Many contemporary theories of humour are variations on the superiority theory, the release theory, the play theory, and, most frequently, the incongruity theory. One extremely interesting and important contemporary theory of humour that breaks with precedent has been offered by Jerrold Levinson, perhaps the leading aesthetician of his generation of Anglo–American philosophers. Indeed, Levinson's theory is so original that it calls for special attention.

According to Levinson, something is humorous just in case it has the disposition to elicit, through the mere cognition of it, and not for ulterior reasons, a certain kind of pleasurable reaction in appropriate subjects (that is, informationally, attitudinally, and emotionally prepared subjects), and where, furthermore, this pleasurable reaction (amusement, mirth) is identified by its own disposition to induce, at moderate or higher degrees, a further phenomenon, namely laughter. Thus, for Levinson, humour cannot be detached from a felt inclination, however faint, towards the convulsive bodily expression of laughter.

This theory can be called the *dispositional theory* of humour insofar as its putatively special insight is that humour involves a disposition towards laughter. Like the incongruity theory, it acknowledges the importance for humour of a cognitive-response element. But Levinson does not define that response as narrowly as the perception of incongruity. Rather, he leaves uncharacterized the nature of the relevant cognitions and their intentional objects, requiring only that said cognitions have some intentional object towards which they are directed and, in addition, he demands that they elicit pleasure for its own sake from suitable percipients.

Of course, this much of Levinson's analysis could be satisfied by mathematical theorems of sufficient cleverness where an elegant solution precipitates a welling up of intellectual pleasure. In order to forestall counter examples like this one, Levinson's final requirement is that the pleasure elicited by the cognition of the humorous be identified by its own disposition to induce laughter; for, though mathematical ingenuity may provoke laughter for some, it has no reliable disposition to do so, even among the mathematicians who take pleasure in it.

Although Levinson's theory locates humour in a certain kind of pleasure, he does not give us much by way of a characterization of the nature of that pleasure. By suggesting that it is mirth or amusement, the definition appears to flirt with the kind of circularity one finds in definitions of Molière's 'dormitive power of sleep' variety. (In *The Imaginary Invalid*, when one character asks why opium causes sleep, he is told that it is in virtue of its dormitive power.)

In order for the theory to be of any use in identifying humour, Levinson needs to link the unspecified feelings of pleasure that he has in mind to their disposition to elicit laughter. Thus, given Levinson's account, it is the disposition to elicit laughter, laughter grounded in pleasurable cognitions, upon which we must rely in order to hive off humour from committed puzzle solving. Laughter, as the ordinary language philosophers of yesteryear might have put it, is the component of Levinson's theory 'that wears the trousers.'

This disposition towards laughter, moreover, need not be intense. It may be only a faint inclination, and, of course, it need not actually find expression in overt laughter. It can be nothing more than an impulse in that direction. This is a dispositional theory, since it does not, like the incongruity theory, specify anything about the structure of the intentional object of comic amusement, but only demands that whatever pleasures the cognitions give rise to have the further disposition, however slight, to elicit laughter.

It is not evident how strictly Levinson intends us to understand the notion of a disposition towards laughter. Some invented humour is very low key. It invites an extremely mild, but none the less real, sense of pleasure that, at best, manifests itself in a brief, almost undetectable, smile or maybe nothing more than a twinkle of the eye. Are we to regard this as a felt, albeit faint, inclination towards laughter? Ordinarily, I think we would not, though perhaps Levinson should be allowed either to stipulate that any slight, physically manifested, impulses in the direction of risibility count as laughter, or else to rewrite his theory in terms of any slight inclinations to laughter or smiles of any sort, including very discreet and very transitory ones.

Nevertheless, there is a problem with both of these alternatives. Both, like Levinson's original proposal, connect humour *necessarily* to certain kinds of bodies—paradigmatically human

45

bodies. Thus communities of telepathically communicating brains in vats, disembodied gods, and aliens without the biological accoutrements to support laughter or even smiling could not be said by us to have humour as a feature of their societies. But I am not convinced that our ordinary concept of humour is so restrictive. We would not charge a science fiction writer with conceptual incoherency if they imagined an alien society of the sort just mentioned and also described it as possessing humour.

Standardly, we grant that there are pleasures, such as certain aesthetic and/or intellectual pleasures, that do not involve any distinctive bodily sensations. Suppose a community of disembodied gods enjoyed incongruities but did not laugh, because they lacked the physical equipment. Would we say there was no humour there, even though they create, exchange, and enjoy things that look like jokes, even if we don't get them? Remember that these jokes give them pleasure—pleasure akin to certain aesthetic or intellectual pleasure—though without laughter or the inclination thereto. It does not appear to be self-contradictory or a conceptual mistake to imagine disembodied spirits being comically amused. Nor does it seem open to Levinson to reject these counter examples because they are imagined rather than actual, since his theory appears to aspire to discover the essence of comic amusement in every conceivable world setting.

Furthermore, consider a community of humans who, as a result of grave cervical cord injuries, lack the ability to move air owing to the inhibition of the muscles in their diaphragm, thorax, chest, and belly. These people cannot laugh, since they do not possess the necessary motor control to respirate, or even to feel any of the pressures that dispose 'normals' towards laughter. Let us also imagine that their faces are so paralysed that they cannot even begin to smile. Nevertheless, they surely, like the gods, could create, exchange, and enjoy in-jokes that we outsiders might not get, but that we can still recognize as jokes, either on formal grounds or because the injured jokesters tell us. Would we say that this society lacked humour?

My intuition is to answer 'no' in the cases of such disembodied gods, biologically alien aliens, and injured humans, because I do not think that our concept of humour necessarily requires an inclination towards laughter, though admittedly laughter is a regularly recurring concomitant of humour among standard-issue human beings. Yet if the laughter stipulation is dropped from Levinson's definition, he will, unlike certain versions of the incongruity theory, have no way to exclude puzzle solutions from the domain of humour, since he has left the structure of the intentional object of comic amusement wide open. Nor can he say without appearing to beg the question that the type of pleasure afforded by puzzles is necessarily not humour.

Levinson does not specify the nature of the cognitions requisite for humour because he feels that specification—of the sort one finds in the incongruity theory—may be too exclusive. He does not, though, offer any compelling counter examples to the incongruity theory. The one brief case that he discusses is that of someone slipping on a banana peel, but, in acknowledging that this may be humorous in that it involves a deflation of expectations, or strangeness or surprise, Levinson makes the case sound more like an exemplification of a generous notion of incongruity rather than a counter instance. Bergson, of course, would analyse such an example as a matter of mechanical absentmindedness—a deviation from the norm of properly functioning sentience—and therefore as an incongruity. Consequently, it is not clear that Levinson has a persuasive reason to avoid specification of the relevant cognitions in terms of perceived incongruity, or else something like it—perhaps some refined successor notion.

One reason to suspect Levinson's liberalism about the scope of the cognitions he allows with respect to humour is the following counter example. Certain avant-garde films, such as those of Jean-Luc Godard, contain allusions to other works of art—not only other films, but paintings, etc. When suitably prepared viewers—the cognoscenti, if you will—detect those allusions, they laugh in order to advertise or signal their pleasure in recognizing the reference. This is quite customary, as can be confirmed by frequenting any avant-garde film venue. But the allusions need not be funny or humorous. They obviously engage cognition, directed at the allusion, whose recognition gives rise to pleasure, which in turn disposes cinéphiles towards laughter—a disposition that is often manifested. Granted, some of these allusions may be humorous in the ordinary sense; but they need not be. And where the allusion is not itself funny in context, it seems wrong to call it humorous, although Levinson will have to.

Moreover, the problem here is not restricted to just this single type of counter example. Recent scientific research on laughter has found that most laughing in everyday life does not occur after jokes or funny remarks, but as a kind of conversational lubricant in ordinary discourse. For example, note the frequent small bursts of laughter that accompany the exchanges between interlocutors during an interview programme on the radio. Moreover, this feature of everyday laughter constitutes a formidable problem for Levinson's theory, since, as a matter of fact, laughter often follows upon pleasures engendered by cognitions that are not comic in nature (e.g. cognitions about a couple's plans to become engaged). But surely not every sort of phatic laughter, issuing from ordinary cognitions, signals humour.

The incongruity theory revisited

Traditional theories of humour and the more recent dispositional theory all have their share of difficulties. However, the incongruity theory still seems the most promising, because it offers the most informative approach to locating the structure of the intentional object of comic amusement. This allows us to employ it productively in comic analysis—enabling us to pinpoint and to dissect the designs that give rise to amusement in jokes, plays, satires, sitcoms, etc. For example, we can begin to isolate what makes a joke funny by locating the perceived incongruity (or incongruities) to which it compels attention. Perceived incongruity, in other words, gives us a leg up on comprehending humour.

Of course, current versions of the incongruity theory may seem unsatisfactory, because the notion of incongruity is simply too elastic. But perhaps some of that elasticity can be alleviated by supplementing the idea of incongruity with elements from the other leading theories.

Both the release theory and the dispositional theory of humour include an experiential dimension in their accounts of comic amusement. Many release theories and Levinson's dispositional theory are vulnerable to criticism on the grounds that the experiences they invoke are tied to specific physiological states, frequently ones that are hypothetical. Nevertheless, the notion of tying comic amusement to certain common experiences is clearly an idea worth exploring.

Of course, the version of the incongruity theory presented earlier had an experiential dimension. We conjectured that comic amusement involved enjoyment, enjoyment spurred by the movement of mind, which quickens and then deciphers the incongruity. But taking a cue from our discussion of release theories, we may also add that that experience is also coloured by the quality that we have labelled 'levity,' an experience that accompanies the disappearance of a cognitive demand into nonsense—a.k.a. Kant's 'nothing.' That is, upon being confronted with an incongruity, we begin to rally ourselves to meet a potential challenge, but assessing the stimulus to be an absurdity we relax our guard or lighten up, thereby undergoing an experience of levity (or lightness).

So provisionally, let us say that creatures like us are in a state of comic amusement just in case (i) the object of one's mental state is a perceived incongruity which (ii) one regards as non-threatening or otherwise anxiety producing, and (iii) not annoying and (iv) towards which one does not enlist genuine problem-solving attitudes (v) but which gives rise to enjoyment of precisely the pertinent incongruity and (vi) to an experience of levity. And humour then is the response-dependent object of comic amusement, characterized thus.

As indicated earlier, theories of this sort have been propounded at least since the 18th century and have, as a result, been taxed by a number of recurring objections. So, before concluding this chapter, let me attempt to address some of these challenges.

The first objection, which hails from the well-known philosopher and polemicist Roger Scruton, is that perceived incongruity is not a necessary condition for comic amusement. Consider the case of caricature. For example, political caricatures of Richard Nixon often emphasized his five o'clock shadow in order to underscore his thuggishness. Supposing that this caricature reveals something true about the character of Richard Nixon—that is, something that corresponds to the way things are—then you might be tempted to say that what we enjoy here are congruities, rather than incongruities.

A second counter example, in a similar vein, observes that we may be comically amused when someone acts in a way that is hypertrophically in character—for instance, a miser who is so cheap that, despite his great wealth, he walks twenty miles instead of paying one pound for public transportation. Again, the point here is that this behaviour is extremely congruous with the miser's character or what we expect of it, a truth, so to speak, about his very nature. Therefore, incongruity is not a necessary condition for comic amusement.

Perhaps needless to say, I am very suspicious about these counter examples. I think that ultimately they rely upon playing fast and loose with our operative understandings of 'incongruity' and 'congruity.' That is, equivocation is afoot here. In the case of caricature, the alleged 'congruity' is 'truth with respect to the subject's character.' Yet this sort of *congruity*, if that's what you call it, is perfectly compatible with the sort of incongruity that is relevant to visual caricature—specifically, deviations from the appearance of the subject, most often in terms of exaggeration (as is apparent in the emphasis placed on outsized ears in political cartoons of LBJ, George W. Bush, and Barack Obama). One doubts that there would be comic amusement without these perceived incongruities, since revealing self-portraits, such as those of Rembrandt, do not evoke comic amusement. Why not? Because there's nothing *visually* incongruous about them.

A similar strategy may help us dissolve problems like that of the miser. The miser's behaviour is said to be revelatory of his true character. Yet this is consistent with the behaviour being incongruous due to his exaggerated thriftiness. It goes way beyond any reasonable norms of prudence. The behaviour is hyperbolic, and hyperbole is a form of incongruity.

Still another set of counter examples are intended to show that incongruity is not sufficient for comic amusement. These counter examples are meant to show that incongruity theorists fail to differentiate comic amusement from certain other of the kinds of pleasure that we may take when engaging with artworks.

One of the pleasures to be had from watching and thinking about Orson Welles's film *Citizen Kane* rests upon trying to interpret the central contradiction in the story: Is a human life, like Kane's, unfathomable or can it be explained by clues as pregnant as 'Rosebud'? Isn't a large measure of the enjoyment that we derive from *Citizen Kane* a function of the hermeneutic play in which we are encouraged to immerse ourselves when tracking the significance of the narrative? But even if we call this amusement, it is not comic amusement, as we usually apply that concept. Therefore, the incongruity theory of comic amusement is too broad.

Also, many surrealist images, such as Dali's melting timepieces, intrigue us by means of their incongruity. Yet paintings like these do not prompt comic amusement. They are far too ominous. So once again the incongruity theory is not tight enough.

Undoubtedly, these objections have a great deal of force against very rudimentary incongruity theories of comic amusement—theories that simply define the state of comic amusement as a response to perceived incongruity. But the version of the incongruity theory that we have fielded possesses resources capable of containing these objections. The surrealist incongruities are intended to be unsettling. Unlike jokes, they do not even counterfeit a patina of intelligibility. They defy intelligible explanation, and they do not support even faux intelligible explanations. They are designed to disturb—to elicit a haunting sense of enigma or mystery. And in that regard they are excluded from the order of comic amusement on my account, because they are anxiety producing.

Responses to artworks that involve interpretive play, on the other hand, are typically enjoyable. Reflecting upon *Citizen Kane* and discerning a theme that may unify its disparate elements can be enjoyable. But notice here that the pleasure is connected to our adoption of a genuine problem-solving attitude; it is grounded in working out the interpretation. Thus it is excluded by the preceding definition from counting as comic amusement. Likewise, incongruity of metaphors and other figures of speech in poetry and other forms of literature are not counter examples, because they invite genuine interpretation, which is a form of problem solving.

One last objection points out that repetition often incites comic amusement, but is not necessarily incongruous. That is true, but then again not all repetition is comically amusing. The repetitions that strike us as comic are typically connected to one or another form of incongruity. In *Monty Python* the phrase 'And now for something completely different' is often repeated. But it is not just the repetition that is funny here. It is the fact that in this case we have what is actually a non sequitur masquerading as a legitimate connective.

There is also a famous vaudeville skit in which every time a character hears the phrase 'Niagara Falls,' he turns murderously upon whoever said it and begins to intone the narrative of how he dealt with his unfaithful wife and her lover, starting with the words 'Slowly I turned....' What is humorous in this routine is the utter incongruity of this behaviour in context, given that the person upon whom the narrator turns had nothing to do with the wife. Of course, sometimes the repetition of a phrase can make us giddy, but usually when the phrase is being repeated with multiple meanings, after the fashion of a pun, and/or because of the improbability of the same formula returning so often in a 'straight' conversation.

Moreover, repetition in diverse contexts can evoke mirth insofar as the same word or situation type will activate different conceptual and neural networks, thereby provoking contrasting and potentially incongruous juxtapositions.

It may seem as though these responses to the question of repetition merely reopen a more enduring charge against the incongruity theory of comic amusement, namely that incongruity is too vague a concept to be of much use. Insofar as there is some justice to that claim, I recommend that we only embrace the incongruity theory provisionally as the best way to advance the discussion. Let us employ the notion of incongruity in our future research as a heuristic which, though slippery, is not vacuous, and apply it to a wide number of cases in the hope of isolating, as exactly as possible, the pertinent recurring variables in the leading structures of humour. For using incongruity in this way, it may function as a serviceable stratagem—indeed, the most useful one we have so far—for unearthing the mechanisms that drive the various comic genres such as jokes and comic plots.

So, let the reader test this hypothesis by using the notion of perceived incongruity and the many examples of it in this chapter as a means for parsing the episodes of humour they encounter on a daily basis. Take note of the frequency that pinpointing the perceived incongruity in a specimen of humour enables one to dissect it, so to speak, at its joints.

Chapter 2
Humour, emotion, and cognition

So far, we have been treating comic amusement—the state to which humour gives rise—as an emotional state. This assumption is unproblematic with respect to the superiority theory of humour, since according to that view comic amusement is a matter of contempt, and contempt is straightforwardly an emotional state. But I have been recommending the adoption of an incongruity theory of comic amusement. Is comic amusement an emotional state given the sort of incongruity theory that we are presently advising?

Emotion/amusement analogies

Clearly, there are a number of correlations between comic amusement and paradigmatic emotional states. First, both are directed. Fear is directed at things *perceived* to be threatening; comic amusement, in turn, is directed at the humorous, which, according to the theory under examination, is that which is necessarily typically *perceived* to be incongruous. The object that fear is directed at is intentional, by which I mean that it need not exist. It is something that is perceived to be threatening, but may not be. Indeed, it may not even be real. Likewise, the object of comic amusement is perceived to be incongruous, but need not be.

Amusement comes in degrees, as do the paradigmatic emotions, and it is subject to a measure of self-control; I can control my amusement to a certain extent, just as I can control my fear and anger somewhat. As well, I can be self-deceived about the source of my enjoyment with respect to hearing a joke, just as I might be self-deceived about my attitude towards a co-worker of mine who happens to be of another race or sexual persuasion.

Another correspondence between comic amusement and typical emotional states is that both would appear to have a formal object, that is, a criterion of appropriateness that governs the mobilization of the state. A necessary condition for being in the state of fear is that one perceives the particular object in question as dangerous or harmful. If I am of sound mind and body, I cannot be in the state of fear unless I perceive the object of that state to be harmful. It may not be dangerous, but I must perceive it to be so. Here, perceived harmfulness is the formal object or criterion of appropriateness for the emotion of fear.

Likewise, on the superiority theory of comic amusement, the formal object of my state is that which I perceive to be inferior to me, while, on the incongruity theory, the formal object is that which seems to me (or which I apprehend and appraise as) incongruous.

Also, once a paradigmatic emotion is up and running, it cognitively takes over the situation in which we find ourselves and spotlights features of the context that reinforce the animating affective state. If we are angry with our partner, the anger will enable us to find more things to be angry about (think about how all those arguments with your lover tend to escalate). Similarly, when we are comically amused, we will be inclined towards finding more absurdities in the circumstances. One bon mot elicits others. Remembering one aspect of a silly event or character from the past calls forth the remembrance of other silly aspects, either from ourselves or from other listeners who are privy to the same history.

Sometimes emotions can inaugurate mood states—mental attitudes which calibrate perception and memory to process everything under their aegis. When one is joyful, for example, everything takes on a happy cast. The grumpy old man next door appears quaint rather than nasty. Analogously, sustained comic amusement can put us in a comic mood, one in which we perceive something incongruous in everything that comes our way. This is especially evident with respect to comic plays and movies where instances of mirth in the opening segments of the narrative put us in a jocular state of mind that not only primes us for future witticisms but also disposes us to laugh where we otherwise might not—at some quirk of the actor, a wayward glance, or an unfamiliar line reading.

Another important feature of the emotions is that they are highly infectious. Psychologists refer to this as 'emotional contagion.' As is readily observable, anger can rapidly course through a mob. But the same is true of comic amusement. It is often observed that people are more likely to laugh out loud in a cinema with an audience than when they are watching the same film at home alone. Indeed, we speak of 'infectious laughter.' Moreover, it is because the producers of sitcoms were aware of this effect that they began putting laugh tracks on TV comedies, beginning on 9 September 1950 with *The Hank McCune Show* and made famous by series such as America's *I Love Lucy*. It is a common practice, employed, for instance, in programmes such as *Benny Hill* and it continues into the present.

Yet despite these correlations and others, a number of objections have been advanced against the idea that comic amusement is an emotion and, it seems fair to say, these objections have been made with the incongruity theory of humour in mind.

Denying that comic amusement is an emotional state

An initial objection to the hypothesis that comic amusement is an emotional state is that the emotions involve an alteration of one's body and/or state, but it is not clear that comic amusement necessarily does so. This may sound strange. If any state is associated with bodily change, surely comic amusement is, since it is usually manifested by explosive laughter. But, as we have seen, although laughter is a frequent correlate of comic amusement, it is not invariant. Sometimes a witticism will tease no more from us than a slight smile or a mild tug at the edge of our lips. But these are still bodily transformations and should be sufficient to at least begin to blunt the objection.

And, in addition, even where these are not in evidence, I suggest, borrowing as I did from relief theories in the previous chapter, that there is, nevertheless, at least typically in creatures like us, a palpable feeling that accompanies comic amusement which we may call levity and which we may describe phenomenologically as a sudden feeling of lightness, a tendency to quicken and then relax. It involves at least a psychological feeling of being unburdened—of tightening up (as in 'uptight') in the face of a potential difficulty, and then letting go. For example, we feel the pressure of puzzlement upon hearing the punchline of a joke, which then dissipates pleasantly when the silliness it signifies dawns upon us. That is, a phenomenological sense of tensing or being set aback when confronted by a humorous absurdity is then followed by a psychological feeling of settling back, or ease, or relaxation when we realize it presents no challenge. This ensuing experience of levity, I contend, is an essential feature of comic amusement and the psychological transition it marks is sufficient to categorize the process as an emotional one.

Another objection to the notion that comic amusement is an emotion is that the emotions, properly so called, paradigmatically require beliefs in order to ignite, but nobody believes that there exists anyone as dumb as the moron. And related to the idea that genuine emotions are connected to beliefs is the supposition that all of the emotions are action guiding. They motivate us to behave in certain ways. Fear prepares us to fight, flee, or freeze. However, comic amusement does not motivate us to move in one direction or another. When comically amused, we enjoy what appears to us to be a harmless incongruity, but we feel no impulse to do anything about it.

These objections both fail in two ways: in their presumptions about the nature of the emotions in general and in their presumptions about comic amusement in general. With respect to the emotions in general, not all emotions require beliefs. Emotional responses to fictional characters and events need not rest upon beliefs. I can feel sorrow for Anna Karenina, although I do not believe that she exists since I know that she and all of the events that befall her were made up by Leo Tolstoy.

Emotions need not be rooted in beliefs in the existence of the persons, places, and events at which they are aimed (where beliefs, here, are understood as propositions held before the mind as asserted). Genuine emotions may issue from imaginings, construed as propositions or situation types entertained or supposed non-assertively. When reading *Gone with the Wind*, for example, I entertain the proposition that 'Scarlett O'Hara lived at Tara,' but not as an assertion; for as Sir Philip Sidney said with respect to poetry, a fiction affirms nothing.

Nor are fictions the only examples of emotions born of imagining. You can certainly engender anxiety in yourself by fancying your finger being cut off in a meat-slicing machine, even though you know and therefore believe that there is no such device in the vicinity.

Consequently, because genuine emotions can issue from imaginings, the fact that much humorous incongruity, as is the case with most jokes, is fictional or made up (and imagined rather than believed by the audience) provides no reason to dismiss the claim that comic amusement is an emotional state.

Nor would it help matters to speculate that when the paradigmatic emotions are discharging their paradigmatic function, they are tied to beliefs. For certainly the fact that our prehistoric forebears were capable of being frightened by contrary-to-fact stories about what could happen to them—as opposed to what they believed was happening to them—performed an advantageous evolutionary function. It kept many children out of places—such as those where alligators were known to congregate—where they might otherwise have been devoured without ever having the opportunity to reproduce.

However, the no-belief argument against the suggestion that comic emotion is an emotion falters not only because the emotions do not require beliefs. It also supposes that comic amusement may never rest upon beliefs. But when watching *Monty Python* and laughing at John Cleese performing one of his silly walks, I don't imagine that he is walking incongruously; I *believe* that he is walking incongruously. And when I see an outlandish hat and smile, I believe that the hat is outlandish and I don't just suppose it is so.

Furthermore, the fact that our comic amusement can be connected to our beliefs has ramifications for the claim that comic amusement motivates nothing. Satire is an important source of comic amusement. The San Francisco Mime Troupe and the American countercultural troupe Bread and Puppet Theater, in the tradition of Bertolt Brecht, employ satire in order to change our beliefs. They use a trope of comic incongruity—specifically hyperbole—for the purpose of influencing our beliefs about the *establishment* in the hope that this will dispose us to certain forms of political action, if only electoral action. Surely, the British film *In the Loop* was intended to undermine our trust in—our belief in—policymakers and diplomats and there is no reason to suppose that it did not work its rhetoric successfully on some viewers. Indeed, satirizing sexism, racism, and/or homophobia may alter our beliefs in ways that may change our own behaviours. And, in any event, much cultural work has been predicated on this belief.

Of course, the no-motivation argument also depends upon a faulty generalization about the emotions. Not all emotional states incline us towards action. As an academic, I may feel great sorrow that the Great Library of Alexandria was destroyed by fire, but that sadness over the loss of that treasure trove of ancient wisdom does not motivate me to do anything. After all, there is nothing that I can do about it but grieve. Nor does this sorrow dispose me towards even wishing that the library was never aflame, since I realize that that would have shifted the course of history in unforeseeable but potentially unhappy ways. Thus, my grief prompts me neither to act nor even to wish I could act. Not all emotional states are motivating. Consequently, even were it the case that comic amusement never motivates us to action, that would fail to show it is not an emotional state.

John Morreall, the philosopher who has probably written more than any other contemporary philosopher about comic amusement, has advanced a somewhat more complicated objection to the claim that comic amusement is an emotion. He argues that with the emotions, properly so called, when we find the emotional state in question pleasurable, we simultaneously find the object of the emotional state pleasing. When we are in the state of requited love, for example, our overall condition is pleasurable and we are pleased by our beloved. When we are frightened by a snake, our state is one of distress and we are distressed by the snake.

But this kind of symmetry can be lacking in cases of comic amusement. In order to flesh out this objection, Morreall develops the following example: 'Amusement...is pleasant not in that the thing which amuses us is pleasing to us—often amusing objects are unattractive and even potentially repulsive—but in that our observing it or thinking about it is a pleasant experience. The gaily painted house with the odd windows, for instance, may strike us as grotesque; what is pleasant is seeing it among the other houses with which it obviously doesn't belong. What amuses us is the incongruity of the house in this setting.'

Let us call this the symmetry argument. Like the no-belief and no-motivation arguments, however, it presupposes a generalization about the emotions which does not hold across the board. Contempt is an emotion, but clearly one can enjoy feeling contempt for something—one can be pleased by looking down at it—without being pleased by the object of our contempt. Morreall feels amused by the gaudy house in his example. Someone less tolerant than Morreall might feel contempt in the same circumstances. The experience of contempt can be quite gratifying. Many enjoy being members of cliques that disparage outsiders and their taste. There is no question that contempt is an emotional state, although there need be no symmetry between the potential pleasure of the experience of feeling contempt and the aversion or repulsion felt by those who are contemptuous towards those whom they find contemptible. Consequently, there should be no problem where there is an asymmetry between the experience of comic amusement and its objects. After all, the superiority theory is mostly about contempt and we have conceded that the feelings it tracks pertain to a great deal of humour.

Roger Scruton, whom we encountered in the previous chapter, denies that comic amusement can be an emotion, on the grounds that it lacks a formal object or criterion of appropriateness. Of course, I have maintained that perceived incongruity, appropriately qualified, is the formal object of or standard of appraisal pertaining to comic amusement. Scruton challenges this for several reasons.

First, he maintains that incongruity is not a necessary condition for comic amusement. You will recall that it was his argument that we encountered in the preceding chapter which alleged that comic amusement often issues—as in the case of caricature—from *congruity* rather than incongruity.

Second, he suggests that rather than being a pattern of thought that perceives things in an incongruous light, comic amusement is a devaluing mode of attending to things. Humour is a form of belittling. Moreover, Scruton suspects we will not be able to turn the notion of a devaluing pattern of attention into a formal object. Scruton never shows why this cannot be done. His sole evidence that comic amusement always devalues appears to be that no one allegedly enjoys being laughed at.

As I hope that I have already demonstrated, Scruton's rejection—on the basis of the notion of comic congruities—of incongruity as the formal object of the relevant variety of amusement relies upon equivocation. In the case of graphic caricature, the equivocation is between congruity-as-correspondence-to-the-nature-of-its-subject versus incongruity-as-lack-of-correspondence-to-the-appearance-of-its-subject. Surely, these are not incompatible. Both may obtain with respect to the same figures. Moreover, if only the former variety of congruity occurred without the discrepancy in appearance, there would be no comic amusement. Think of those photographs of Winston Churchill as a mountain of smouldering determination. They reveal the resoluteness in his character, but they are not funny. They are not caricatures, precisely because they are not visually incongruous.

As a rival to the conjecture that comic amusement involves perceiving things in an incongruous light, Scruton proposes that comic amusement involves seeing things in a devaluing light. Comic amusement is a form of attentive demolition. Scruton doesn't think that this conception will yield a formal object because there are so many different ways of thinking about things in a devaluing manner. I am not sure why this preludes there being a formal object in the neighbourhood, since there are so many *different* ways to fear things, to be angered by things, and, for that matter, to find something incongruous about them.

Moreover, not all philosophers agree that the emotions proper require formal objects. For some, such as Amelie Rorty and

63

Patricia Greenspan, the emotions may merely involve patterns of attention. And Scruton's notion of devaluation certainly sounds like a pattern of attention. Thus, his argument will not persuade philosophers such as Greenspan and Rorty.

However, my deeper reservations concerning Scruton's proposal is that the alternative he offers to incongruity does not fare as well as incongruity when weighed against the data. That is, supposing that Scruton's congruity arguments have not banished the incongruity theory from the contest, incongruity is more comprehensive than Scruton's candidate. For, as we have seen, sometimes comic amusement arises when we encounter something that deviates from a norm but in a way that excels. When Buster Keaton manipulates the things of the world with unsurpassed ingenuity, grace, and wit, our giddiness is not a matter of attentive demolition but of attentive admiration.

Scruton's evidence for the hypothesis of attentive demolition is that no one wants to be laughed at. But I'm not completely convinced of this. Certainly professional comics—especially those who specialize in self-deprecation, such as the American Rodney Dangerfield—want to be laughed at; they would be out of business otherwise. And, as I recall from my own youth, class clowns are quite happy to do anything for a laugh.

Of course, Scruton may protest that by 'being laughed at,' he just means 'being devalued in a way no one wishes to be.' Yet certainly being laughed at may have the more innocent meaning of 'being the particular object of comic amusement,' as in the case of Buster Keaton performing some ingenious feat. But, in that event, it may be that Scruton is begging the question. What he has proven is not that comic amusement is always tantamount to belittling attention, but merely that some instances of 'laughing at someone' are derisive. However, that is hardly enough upon which to mount a theory.

The neo-Jamesian objection

A more recent kind of objection to the notion on the table—that comic amusement is an emotional state directed at incongruities—may be that it is too cognitive. It would appear to presuppose something like a cognitive theory of the emotions. On the incongruity theory, the comically amused subjects marshal categories, attempt to subsume the object of amusement under said categories, and then enjoy the way or ways in which it slips out of them.

Yet on neo-Jamesian views, of the sort that are steadily gaining traction nowadays, there seems to be too much thinking going on here. As with their forebear and namesake, the philosopher and psychologist William James, for the neo-Jamesians an emotional state is much more like a perception than a cognitive categorization process. It is a non-cognitive, affective appraisal which then elicits a physiological change. Where cognition enters the picture is after the original response, when it functions to monitor and modify the earlier and ongoing stages of our response. Were comic amusement an emotional state, it might be argued, it would not be as intellectual as the incongruity theory of comic amusement presumes. Consequently, comic amusement, if it is analysed by means of the incongruity theory, is not an emotional state.

As a first response, let me protest that even though I accept the scientific evidence that something like the aforesaid scenario describes the most frequent pattern of emotional response, I do not see why neo-Jamesians are so convinced that emotional states never take the trajectory hypothesized by earlier cognitive theories of the emotions. In these theories, some cognitive-evaluative interlude precedes the physiological-feeling stage of the emotion. Aren't some emotions like that, such as academic envy?

Furthermore, it seems to me that various neo-Jamesian attempts to accommodate these, more apparently cognitively driven, emotional states are suspiciously ad hoc. Jenefer Robinson, the leading neo-Jamesian aesthetician, claims that where deliberation precedes affective appraisal, there is an intervening stage during which our emotional memory system matches our deliberation with previous scenarios or situational types, which memories then elicit bodily appraisals. And this—the bodily appraisal stage—is where the emotion proper starts.

But, to me, there seems to be an extra step here. Why can't deliberation alone arrive at an appraisal sufficient to provoke a physiological change? Why do we have to be rerouted through emotively charged memory types? It strikes me that only the commitment to a thoroughgoing non-cognitivism makes the move tempting, which, in this context, would amount to presupposing what needs to be shown. So, for the moment at least, I think it is fair to assume that some emotional states are structured in the way earlier cognitive theories of the emotions suggested and that at least *some* cases of comic amusement can be understood on this model.

Yet what of the remaining cases? Here I think that the incongruity theory of comic amusement need not be thought to be as categorically inhospitable to neo-Jamesianism as may have been suggested thus far.

In order to see how this may be so, consider the two-stage structure of most jokes. For example:

> Beth calls her friend James from the motorway on her cell phone. Beth tells James to be careful, because the radio says there is a nut on the motorway driving in the wrong direction. James says, 'Yeah, there are hundreds of them.'

Stage one of the joke is completed when the punchline arrives. Punchlines are by nature puzzling. They call for interpretations. Stage two occurs when the listener reaches the interpretation.

But the interpretation is generally as incongruous or absurd as the punchline. In the preceding joke, the punchline prompts or at least nudges listeners to ask how there could be hundreds of people on the motorway driving in the wrong direction. Then we realize that James is the nut who is driving against the traffic. Yet it is nearly inconceivable—it strains the principle of interpretive charity to breaking point—to imagine that there is someone so dimwitted that he fails to see that he is driving the wrong way on a crowded motorway. Such a person would be as nonsensical as the moron. In fact, James is the moron.

This scenario, however, fits very neatly with the neo-Jamesian characterization of the emotions. At stage one, there is an affective appraisal. Following the neo-Jamesian scenario, let us say it amounts to something like the apprehension 'This is strange and unexpected,' or 'This is unusual,' or maybe even 'This is incongruous.' That is, the affective appraisal stage involves pattern recognition, which, of course, will also be sensitive to deviations from the pattern. This may lead to the physiological state we may call 'being taken aback.' As researchers have observed, this will activate the sympathetic-medullary system (SAM), which primes the initiation of the fight/flight response. But then this sequence is subjected to cognitive monitoring, which establishes the absence of threat and identifies the stimulus as harmless nonsense. Since it is harmless, the emotion is not fear. Since it is nonsensical, we do not hunker down rationally to figure out this anomaly or to explain it away. Instead we enjoy it, and that enjoyment is signalled either by laughter or a feeling of levity as our initial sense of being taken aback evaporates.

Although the incongruity theory of comic amusement may appear to depend exclusively upon the kind of cognitive theory of the emotions that neo-Jamesians eschew, it need not. In fact, it can be segued nicely with neo-Jamesianism. So, if neo-Jamesianism is true, that is no reason to discount the proposition that comic amusement is an emotional state, understood in terms of incongruity. On the other hand, if some cognitive theory of the emotions or some combination of a cognitive theory and neo-Jamesianism is true, then the incongruity theorist of comic emotion has even less cause for anxiety.

What vital human interests does humour serve?

The last objection to the conjecture that comic amusement is an emotional state is that the emotions involve vital human interests. Fear protects us from harm and anger from injustice. Jealousy warns us that an important source of affection is being taken from us. Sorrow alerts us to loss. But if comic amusement is an emotion, to what vital human interest is it connected? The superiority theory of comic amusement has an answer to this question. The laughter of sudden glory reinforces our sense of social standing. But if the incongruity theory of comic amusement is a more promising perspective, what vital human interest does taking pleasure in incongruity serve?

One provocative suggestion has been offered by the polymath Jonathan Miller, the neurologist, opera director, and former member of the comedy troupe *Beyond the Fringe*. In a way that is consonant with the incongruity theory of comic amusement, Miller cites the scene in *The Gold Rush* where Chaplin eats his boot (see Figure 3). Miller remarks that it constitutes a 'jarring discrepancy in which an object is suddenly forcefully reclassified by being taken out of the category of the radically inedible and placed into the category of the finely, wonderfully edible ... [T]his scene rejuvenates our sense of what everyday categories are.' Miller argues that by playing with our assumptions, categories, and concepts in this way 'we have prevented ourselves from becoming slaves to the categories we live by.' In this regard, humour is the 'rehearsal and re-establishment of concepts.'

3. Charlie Chaplin, *The Gold Rush*

Expanding on this theme, Miller notes: 'In all procedures of life there are rules of thumb which enable us to go on automatic pilot...We depend on the existence of these categories in order to go about our everyday business. Jokes allow us to stand back from these rules and inspect them.' As a result of this, Miller contends that being comically amused enables us to rehearse and revise the categories that we live by, thereby restoring us to what he calls 'more versatile versions of ourselves.' Thus is comic amusement connected to the serious business of serving our highest interests.

Miller's proposal is very congenial to the incongruity theory of comic amusement. And although I concur with Miller that the service of comic amusement concerns cognition typically through play with our concepts, I am not persuaded that humour has much to do with the production of new and better concepts, as Miller seems to think. I suppose that you could say that comic amusement frees us from the tyranny of everyday norms and concepts. But it doesn't give way to higher sense; it leads to nonsense.

Apart from certain philosophical counter examples, it is difficult to come up with many examples of comic amusement leading to genuine concept revision. But Miller is not talking about philosophical counter examples. He's talking about everyday comic amusement.

A more promising conjecture can be found in *The Society of the Mind* by Marvin Minsky, co-founder of the Artificial Intelligence Laboratory at MIT. Like Miller, Minsky emphasizes the connection between comic amusement and cognition. And like Miller, Minsky maintains that the primary function of humour is to disrupt the heuristics we deploy in everyday life.

For an example of what Minsky has in mind, consider this ancient Chinese anecdote: 'A sage encounters a wealthy man walking in front of his horse. The sage asks him why he isn't riding the animal. The rich man replies "Six legs are faster than four."'—a rule of thumb that generally applies, but, as the anecdote reveals, not always.

For Minsky, we are possessed of a plethora of rules of thumb that we use in order to wend our way through life. But these heuristics are imperfect reasoning routines. They work quickly, but not always accurately. Indeed, these heuristics can go wrong, often in more ways than one. According to Minsky, the function of comic amusement is to apprise us of the many ways that normal thinking and reasoning procedures can derail.

The function of humour is to signal the existence of what Minsky calls 'cognitive bugs.' Analogizing his theory to Freud's, Minsky claims that via humour we are able to build up what amounts to an unconscious cognitive censor that polices everyday thinking and guards us against the wealth of errors our heuristics can induce.

I think that Minsky's approach to comic amusement is superior to Miller's, since Minsky is not under the illusion that comic amusement is a font of superior ideas. Its function is to call our attention to flawed thinking. Yet Minsky's analogy of his view to Freud's notion of the unconscious does not succeed. For Freud, jokes elude the censor. In contrast, Minsky maintains that jokes construct the censor—piece by piece, heuristic misfiring by heuristic misfiring.

Nor is the disanalogy an insignificant one. The source of the pleasure in jokes, on Freud's account, is the lifting of censorship. That is, Freud explains the pleasure in joking in terms of its service to an unconscious id. But Minsky has no cognitive id—probably for the simple reason that a cognitive id would be a contradiction in terms. However, that leaves Minsky with no sufficient role for pleasure in his account.

In fact, I think that the problem here is worse than this. The fact that we take pleasure in comic nonsense would seem to predict the opposite of the construction of Minsky's cognitive censor. Since we enjoy comic incongruities, wouldn't that encourage us to perpetrate them? The more the merrier, so to speak. We don't typically suppress that which gives us pleasure. Since comic incongruities make us happy, wouldn't that dispose us to commit more rather than fewer absurdities? Perhaps this is borne out by the readily observed phenomenon that one joke leads to another.

In this respect, contra Minsky, we would predict that comic amusement is the natural enemy of cognition rather than its benefactor. Plato certainly worried about this with regard to the education of his guardians. He recommended that they should not be encouraged to laugh, because those habituated to laughter are inclined to say or to do anything in order to indulge it, no matter how alien to reason.

If humour is linked to 'cognitive bugs,' as Minsky and the incongruity theorists agree, then what service does comic amusement perform for cognition? Wouldn't the pleasure it engenders reinforce our production of errors rather than diminish it? In short, Minsky's notion of a cognitive unconscious censor leaves unexplained the role of comic enjoyment in service to the interests of cognition.

Although it is true that one typically does not spend a great amount of time dwelling upon a joke or upon other forms of comic incongruity, it is quite common to run the punchline and its interpretation through one's mind a few times in order to savour it. Often people repeat the punchline aloud once or twice in order to replay, in a manner of speaking, the joke or the bon mot a second or third time. Like the moment when the interpretation of the punchline first dawns on us, these replays are suffused with pleasure. The function of the pleasure here, it seems to me, is to encourage us to focus intently upon the comic incongruity.

Translating this into Minsky's language, the pleasure component of comic amusement rivets our attention on the cognitive bugs in play and disposes us to scrutinize them closely in order to know them better so as to avoid them in our activation of the panoply of heuristics, rules of thumb, norms, concepts, scenarios, and schemas that we deploy, for the most part, automatically in everyday life.

As Miller observed, much of our thinking is done 'on automatic pilot.' Humour, in turn, relies upon activating unthinking but familiar patterns of inference, false beliefs, and unwarranted assumptions. The punchline of a joke, for example, dawns upon us like the solution to an algebraic problem, but, at the same time, strikes us as nonsensical. It defies understanding in that it cannot be integrated with what we know of how the world is or should be. Adopting Minsky's language, humour debugs our mental processing routines by ferreting out and foregrounding the weaknesses of our various cognitive shortcuts. Humour does this by rewarding the detection of these defects with the pleasure that attends mirth or comic amusement.

Comic amusement not only brings fallacious assumptions and reasoning to our attention, but also lodges these cognitive glitches in our memory. Furthermore, we enjoy recounting these flaws to others as a way of spreading social information about the mistakes folks like us are liable to make. In both cases, mirth is the mechanism. That is, if the pleasures of comic amusement don't make these defects in our cognitive assumptions and processing unforgettable, comic amusement makes them less forgettable. Think how often some mistake in 'real life' calls to mind a joke that you then feel impelled to tell to others privy to the aforesaid 'real life' mishap.

Comic amusement erupts in the process of discerning the way the cognition/emotive system has misfired. Or, to change metaphors, it is part and parcel of the cognitive cleansing process we undergo—which process is stoked by pleasure.

Of course, evolution rarely attaches pleasure to something unless there is cause. Pleasure is connected to comic incongruities in order to flag the pitfalls to which our mental apparatus is irresistibly prone, as is shown by how easily, as they say, we 'fall for a joke.' Thus, much comic amusement, conceived in terms of incongruities (and especially with regard to jokes), can be seen to be like the other emotions, serving vital human interests, namely our interests in cognitive well-functioning.

As noted in the previous chapter, some theorists regard comic amusement as a form of play. We had reason to suspect that this view is inadequate as a universal theory of humour. However, the play theorists were not wrong in noticing that comic amusement is a frequent form of leisure activity, including byplay among friends and acquaintances and more institutionalized 'plays' by professionals. On our view, the play here is with the cognitive incongruities towards which our mental make-up disposes us. Thus, if play in general frequently has the function of enabling us to practise skills that have models in serious activities, then perhaps trading incongruities sharpens our abilities and the abilities of our interlocutors to detect the kinds of errors to which our heuristically driven mental processing disposes us.

In terms of the notion of cognitive cleansing, the frequent association of comic amusement with laughter is especially suggestive. With laughter, we expel breath from our bodies as opposed to, say, awe, where we inhale deeply. Another affect state in which we exhale violently is disgust. The disgust reaction, of course, was adapted initially to reject noxious elements, such as spoiled meat, from our bodies. Disgust makes us gag on things we automatically identify as toxic and inclines us to spit them out (and in extreme cases to vomit them out). Similarly, laughter is expulsive. Perhaps we can interpret it figuratively as a gesture of casting out cognitive bugs or, at least, refusing to ingest them. In this way, comic laughter participates in alerting us to the presence of cognitive bugs in our heuristics and default modes of reasoning, while, at the same time, our laughter is a signal to our conspecifics that something is awry.

Moreover, if much comic amusement is existentially serviceable for the manner in which it so often draws our attention to local flaws in our ways of thinking, it also at least has the potential global significance of disclosing to the reflective student of humour the frailty of human thinking. In comic amusement, we incessantly relearn how readily we err. *Pace* the superiority theory, comic amusement does not and should not serve as a lever of human arrogance, but instead as an occasion for humility—an opportunity for an appreciation of our human weakness.

In this chapter, we have examined the relation of comic amusement to emotion and cognition in the course of defending the notion that comic amusement is an emotion. Undoubtedly, some readers, encountering this debate, asked themselves: 'Who cares whether or not comic amusement is an emotion? What hangs on it? Why not just say *comic amusement* is *comic amusement* and leave it at that?'

One of my reasons for pursuing this issue is that it is of great heuristic value. We are starting to learn a lot about the emotions (and their relation to cognition). Comic amusement is still very mysterious. Thus, by contemplating comic amusement in terms of current thinking about the emotions, we have been able to put ourselves in a position where we can organize the phenomena and parse the structures of comic amusement as well as ask questions about them with greater clarity than did our predecessors.

Chapter 3
Humour and value

Humour may serve many functions. It can be used to relieve stress, to promote amity among strangers, to dissipate tension within a fractious group, to display intelligence, to castigate injustice, to seduce, and so forth. Inasmuch as it discharges these functions well, humour accrues value. Obviously, there are too many connections between humour and value to be pursued in a short chapter, or even a short book.

Consequently, at this point, I will narrow my purview to a consideration of humour in terms of the fundamental role it performs in social life. Humour, I shall argue, is primarily a source of social information about the norms that govern the cultures that we inhabit—the cultures that are us. Humour, and the comic amusement that attends it, alerts us to the relevant social norms and serves to reinforce them. Indeed, in some cases, humour may even function to *enforce* norms—to serve as a corrective. This is not, of course, to claim that humour is either the original or the sole source of this information, but only that it is a particularly cogent source, undoubtedly because its lessons come wrapped in pleasure.

Cultures are engaged in a constant process of reproducing themselves—their norms and their values (ranging from morals to etiquette). This goal is so important that cultures pursue this end through many, often redundant, channels. Humour is one of those conduits. Needless to say, it is an especially delightful one.

In order for comic amusement to take hold, it requires a background of shared presuppositions. First and foremost, these are shared presuppositions about norms (of intelligence, ethics, and even personal hygiene). When we laugh together, we are in effect acknowledging our membership in a community—a community bound together by the norms presumed by the humour at hand—and, in fact, we are also simultaneously celebrating that community when we assemble for merriment. In this context, our converging laughter serves as a signal to each and all of us that we are bound together by shared assumptions.

Humour, in short, is involved in the construction (or, more aptly, the permanent reconstruction) and maintenance of what we might call an *Us*—the *us* that abides by the pertinent norms. But where there is an *us*, there is typically also a *Them*, against whom the rest of us define ourselves. These *them*, then, are those who deviate (or are alleged to deviate) from the norms commemorated by the comic amusement in which the *us* participate.

The next section of this chapter will be devoted to discussing the role of humour in the construction of communities—constellations of Us versus Them as organized around norms and deviations therefrom. Of course, not all of those who are ostracized as Them are treated fairly when they are reduced to comic butts. Indeed, in some cases, it may be argued that it is immoral to treat certain persons and/or groups of people—such as the disabled, perhaps—as objects of comic amusement and as targets of ridicule.

Thus, the last section of this chapter will deal with the question of the relation of humour to morality, asking: (i) when, if ever, it is morally wrong to indulge in humour directed against others, especially members of oppressed groups (such as those involving race, gender, sexual preference), (ii) whether enjoying such

humour shows one's character to be morally flawed, and
(iii) whether the immorality of jokes, humorous remarks, and
caricatures can render them less funny, or more funny. And in the
process of addressing these questions, we will also consider
whether immorality is simply irrelevant when assaying whether
or not humour is amusing.

In other words, the next section of this chapter will be concerned
primarily with humour as a source of predominantly positive social
(and moral) value, while the succeeding section, by examining the
relation of comic amusement to immorality especially, will explore
the topic of humour and disvalue.

Humour and the reproduction of norms

Towards the end of the last chapter, we hypothesized that a
primary function of humour is to draw our attention to the ways
in which the heuristics, schemas, and rules of thumb that we
employ in order to navigate our way through everyday life can
misfire. These heuristics supply us with shortcuts to the solution
of recurring quandaries. They are faster than rational deliberation
and exceptionally useful for that very reason. Yet they are not
quite as reliable, inasmuch as they are shortcuts. Following
Minsky, we can call the glitches to which our heuristics are prone
'cognitive bugs.' Our claim was that humour is, in large measure,
in the business of making us aware of those cognitive bugs—of
'debugging' us, if you will.

To repeat an example from the first chapter: An obese man, his
surplus flesh rolling over the top of his Bermuda shorts, walks
into a pizza restaurant and orders a pizza with everything on it.
The waiter asks whether the man wants it cut into four slices
or eight. 'Four,' says the customer. 'I'm on a diet.' Here, of course,
the comic butt is relying upon the heuristic that fewer portions of
x correlate with less of x in toto, a useful rule of thumb much of
the time but wildly out of place here. The joke calls our attention

to the 'bug' in this heuristic and exterminates it with laughter. Or, to change metaphors, the humour in this case is a form of cognitive hygiene. As Molière remarked: 'The duty of comedy is to correct men by amusement.'

Invented humour makes us keenly alert to the shortcomings in our cognitive routines insofar as it uses our own minds to entrap us in absurdity. When we hear the punchline of a joke that we understand, our mind leaps rapidly and ineluctably to the silly interpretation that the jokester intends. Although we say that *we* get the joke, it might be more accurate to say that the joke gets *us*—gets us or, better, inveigles us to explain away the incongruous punchline by means of a thought generally no less nonsensical than that which inspired it. Moreover, the joke manages to do this by activating mental procedures we incessantly, and almost automatically, mobilize, but in such a way that the fissures latent within them crack wide open.

The heuristic that upends the pizza customer involves logical reasoning. Here by adopting the heuristic in question, our fanciful dieter violates the norm of right thinking. The error in this case involves applying the wrong heuristic to the situation at hand. Moreover, this is frequently the way with invented humour, not only with respect to logic, but also with respect to ethics.

For instance:

A travelling salesman, hawking magazine subscriptions, is visiting a rural farmhouse. As he finishes his pitch to the family, a pig with two wooden legs limps across the sitting room floor. This prompts the salesman to ask: 'Why does the pig have two wooden legs?'

At that point, paterfamilias says: 'Let me tell about that pig. I was out on the east forty a year or two ago and my tractor turned over. I was pinned beneath it; fuel was dripping onto the ground all around me and it was about to explode. But that there pig, he ran

79

all the way to town and brought the sheriff and his boys out here to rescue me. Let me tell you, that's some pig.'

'Yes,' says the salesman, 'but why does it have two wooden legs?'

'Well, listen, that pig is somethin' else. We wuz all asleep one night when the shades in this here room caught fire. Flames were sweeping through the house. We wuz all dead asleep but that there pig, he smelt the smoke and ran squealing through the house. Woke us all up, he did, and saved the day. Why that pig even ran back into the burning building and dragged Baby Bobby-Joe from his blazing crib to safety. By gosh, there ain't no other pig like that pig.'

'Yeah, yeah,' says the salesman, 'but why does the pig have two wooden legs?'

'Well,' says the farmer, 'a pig that special, you wouldn't want to eat all at once.'

In this joke, a way of thinking about a rare comestible, like a fine wine, appears to have been misapplied to circumstances where gratitude would be more appropriate. Whereas the pizza joke involves a violation of the norms of right logical thinking, the special-pig joke transgresses the norms of right moral thinking. Humour discloses the ways in which people's thinking and, for that matter, their acting can misfire not only with respect to their cognitive norms, narrowly construed, but with respect to the norms that they deploy in every other dimension of life as well. Through the embrace of absurdity or error by the comic butts, and/or by the humorist, and/or by the listeners, or by all three at once (and in every possible combination), humour is devoted to showing us the myriad ways in which many of the various structures of thinking and acting upon which we depend can go awry almost by reflex.

Obviously, for humour to explode into comic amusement, we must be aware that an error has been embraced. And that requires that we possess some standard that signals the presence of one or another cognitive, moral, or other sort of snafu—which standard, moreover, we also share with the humorist and the rest of the appreciative audience. But, of course, there is not just one standard here. There are many. For humour explores the transgression of every sort of norm, including those of reasoning, morality, and etiquette, as well as just about every other kind of criterion of appropriateness pertaining to mind and body—to thought and behaviour—of which we can conceive. However, in order to track the transgression of a norm (a.k.a. an incongruity), one must have command of the norm in question. Audience uptake of a specimen of humour then demands that the humorist and the appreciative audience both share the norms in question, at least imaginatively.

Every instance of invented humour occurs against the background of a great deal of information common to every party involved in the humorous transaction. This background information encompasses everything from facts about nature, society, folklore, including urban (and rural) legends, slang, and you name it. Indeed, the background knowledge can extend to knowledge of genre conventions, as when in Roman Polanski's *Fearless Vampire Killers* the creature of the night explains that he cannot be deterred by a crucifix, since he is Jewish. Yet the most important information that must be shared by all the parties to an episode of comic amusement is that of the norms being jostled.

In order to appreciate moron jokes, the tellers and listeners must share the norms regarding intelligence that the moron flaunts with such mindless abandon. To enjoy the apparent clumsiness of the clown tripping over a stool, we implicitly invoke, along with the rest of the audience, a standard of attentiveness and physical coordination against which the inattentiveness and lack of coordination of the clown compare deficiently.

Both cowardice and recklessness can serve as objects of comic amusement for us, because they deviate from our shared norms of courage. Much humour, including bathroom humour, gravitates around filth, because standards of personal hygiene are among the deepest common norms in a society. That is why dressing up in hobo garb was once thought to be one of the funniest Halloween costumes; that is why mere mention of excreta is rewarded with gales of laughter in elementary school.

Hypocrites, such as Molière's Tartuffe, readily draw laughter from broad and varied theatre audiences because they doubly offend our standards of honesty—hypocrites not only lie but also dissemble about their aversion to lying. Pronounced vulgarity, bad taste, and bad manners (including bad breath) can function as a common source of comic amusement for those with converging codes of etiquette. The greedy and the spendthrift, the laze-about and the workaholic are comic motifs because they exceed the relevant cultural means (in the Aristotelian sense), which advocate, instead, moderate thrift and moderate conscientiousness. Sex, particularly in terms of marriage, can provide an indefinitely large number of opportunities for common laughter, since they are so freighted with rules of behaviour just asking to be transgressed.

Even religion is a serviceable topic for humour, simply because it provides occasions for gods, angels, priests, rabbis, ministers, nuns, and so forth to act irreligiously or to misbehave—to violate the mode of conduct that we suppose is becoming to their station. For example:

> A young priest runs into his abbot's office, shouting 'Come quickly, Jesus Christ is in the chapel!' The abbot and the novice hurry to the church, where they see the Lord Jesus, kneeling before the altar, his hands clasped in prayer. The young man turns to the abbot and asks, 'What should we do?' To which the wise old abbot replies, 'Look busy.'

Initially the abbot's reply seems puzzling and inappropriate. One would expect the two holy men to walk forward and fall on their knees in adoration of their Lord and Saviour. But very quickly listeners realize that the abbot does not regard Christ as his Lord and Saviour but as his boss, indeed one who like a very stereotypical, earthly boss stages surprise inspections in order to spy upon shirkers. Not only does our 'wise old abbot' misapply what we might call the 'boss schema' to the situation, but in doing so he behaves in a way that is incongruously irreligious, overturning our expectations about the way in which a man of God ought to behave.

(Postscript: a downside of the current aggressive wave of atheism is that we'll lose a great source of humour.)

The examples in the preceding three paragraphs could be multiplied indefinitely. But what they already suggest would be confirmed again and again by further examples. Comic amusement depends upon shared norms against which the pertinent incongruities take shape. Very often those shared cultural norms are standards of right thought and right behaviour—shared measures of virtue, if you will—and the violations of those norms are recognizable as vices by those who appreciate the humour. Thus, it seems fair to hazard that, to a crucial degree, that which those who enjoy the same instances of humour share is, significantly, common standards of virtue and vice and of right and wrong—mutually acknowledged criteria of appropriateness and inappropriateness, especially regarding human thought and action. And our laughter, in turn, signals to each and all of us our common commitment to these norms.

Of course, humour is not the origin of these norms, nor is it the most important disseminator of them. Parents, peers, friends, relatives, acquaintances, popular culture (apart from humour), religion, advertisements, and so on all function to put these norms in place and keep them there. What humour does, for the most part, is simply (and sometimes not so simply) to reinforce our command of these norms—to rehearse and perhaps sometimes to refine our access to the pertinent norms and deviations from them.

This constellation of norms also goes by the name of 'culture', and the panoply of norms we embrace that constitutes the culture or subculture to which we belong. Comic laughter in concert with like-minded and like-feeling revellers confirms, reinforces, and celebrates our membership in a community defined by our infectious laughter, our de facto acknowledgement, through comic intercourse with others, of our converging norms (at least for the nonce). In addition, our laughter, through its endorphin-mediated opiate effect, in all likelihood boosts the tendency of comic amusement to facilitate social bonding.

That humour functions to build and to consolidate communities, however ephemeral, should be apparent from the way in which we use it to establish contact with strangers. Trapped in an endless checkout queue at the supermarket, we may aspire to relieve tension and promote geniality by calling our fellow victims' attention to an outlandish headline in some tabloid newspaper, such as 'Michael Jackson Died Three Times!' Similarly, politicians frequently begin a speech with a witticism in order to convince voters that they are one of us—we're all in the same boat, as one might say.

Of course, the 'communities' alluded to above are fugitive, often momentary. Laughing about some ridiculous headline about Michael Jackson is not the basis for a relationship that will last a lifetime. It affords an instant of comity, a spate of relief amongst harried shoppers. But surely it strains credulity to call that a 'community.'

Admittedly, it does. And yet it evinces in small what happens at large when jokes, comic plots, witticisms, bon mots, caricatures, and the like circulate widely, summoning up the same norms, standards, and rules again and again. No one wants to call the participants in a shared snicker in the checkout queue of a supermarket a 'culture' or even a 'subculture.' Yet the accumulation of violations of the same norms relentlessly by jokes, sitcoms, cartoons, everyday puns and japes is indicative of something more than a one-off amusement. Mass humour implies the existence of a larger, mass culture, not in the pejorative sense of that phrase, but in the quantitative sense. If the humour is repeated again and again, and the uptake is statistically broad, it seems legitimate to infer that the communities we are talking about are legitimate communities, full-blooded 'cultures' and 'subcultures.'

Thus, it seems reasonable to postulate that a leading function of humour is to reinforce various cultural constellations by enlisting the norms that exist, indeed, pre-exist, amongst a certain group in such a way that those norms are vindicated repeatedly through the absurdities that result from not respecting them. Humour in this fashion 'pays its way in society,' so to say, by acting as the guardian of the relevant norms. Of course, it does not only patrol the infractions of these norms in the abstract, chiding the moron in all of us. Humour may also serve as a corrective concretely. Satires unmask social absurdities in the here and now.

Humour, where successful, creates communities of laughter. These communities of laughter correspond to communities bonded by certain norms. Humour may not create those norms, but it thrives because those norms exist. In this way, humour functions in the defence of the norm. Humour serves to defend the norm that makes those who abide by the norms in question the culture of an *us*.

(This should not be taken to imply that humour is necessarily conservative, politically speaking, since there can be left-wing humour. However, satire of every stripe must presuppose norms—of justice, intelligence, integrity, and so forth—in order to induce comic amusement in an appreciative audience.)

Perhaps there are some specimens of humour whose appeal is nearly universal. Moron jokes might be one candidate, since there would appear to be no one, who is capable of being comically amused by the antics of the moron, who is excluded from the non-moron community (and since the moron is a fictional being, he is neither excluded from nor included in our circle).

However, much humour is not like this. Very frequently, those inside the community of laughter chortle at the expense of outsiders, outsiders whom the humour paints as deficient in terms of the norms shared by the merrymakers. Sometimes, of course, those excluded from the community deserve ostracism, like the Cold War warriors in the film *Dr Strangelove*. But, equally, quite often our comic butts are treated unjustly or unfairly, as in many cases of ethnic, racist, sexist, and homophobic humour. This common phenomenon, of course, raises questions about the relation of humour to morality—questions to which we now turn.

Humour and morality

In our opening chapter, the review of theories of humour revealed that humour comes in contact with ethics in many ways, a number of which are apt to trouble the moralist (as opposed to the moralizer). Humour often involves ridicule and malice, feelings of superiority, scorn towards infirmity, the transgression of ethical norms, and intentional offensiveness; it may even presuppose a sometimes ethically dubious anaesthesia of the heart—the bracketing of sympathy and moral concern—at least for the creatures of comic fictional worlds. It presents for our delight spectacles of greed, venality, promiscuity, cruelty, gluttony, sloth—in short, every manner of vice. All this is apt to make the moralist nervous.

Throughout history, puritanical types have reappeared to admonish humour. In recent years, the discussion of the ethics of humour has become increasingly prominent, perhaps as a reflection of the tides of political correctness in the larger culture. Racist, ethnic, sexist, ageist, classist, homophobic, and ablist jokes have in some circles provided sufficient reason for losing one's job.

However, before the moralist addresses the question of when it is wrong to indulge one's appetite for humour, one must confront the sceptic who alleges that comic amusement is never morally wrong, because humour is beyond good and evil. Let us call this sceptic 'the amoralist.'

Comic amoralism

One response to the current wave of political correctness might be to recommend that everyone just 'lighten up,' on the grounds that humour is neither moral nor immoral, but rather amoral. Humour is a domain, it might be claimed, where morality has no purchase. Various cultures have days set aside, like the ancient Roman Saturnalia, where conventional morality is suspended and ethics is sent on a holiday. Invented humour, such as jokes, the amoralist suggests, is an analogous category of discourse—a verbal carnival.

What is said in jest stays in jest. It is not morally serious. That's why we defend ourselves from those who take moral offence at our humour by claiming, 'I was only joking'—which means, in effect, 'I am not morally accountable; I am not speaking seriously.' If morality seems traduced by the humorist, it is only for the sake of compounding incongruities and not for the purpose of advocating evil. For the amoralist, it is a category mistake to suppose that indulging in humour is ever immoral. Humour is categorically beyond good and evil.

Undoubtedly, in certain cases the amoralist has a point. Consider the riddle: 'What do you have if you have a lawyer buried up to his neck in sand? Not enough sand.' This joke shouldn't be taken as a recommendation to do away with lawyers. It is just a clever way of dissing lawyers, a group that is not in any way socially disadvantaged but is quite the opposite. The case is not as straightforward, however, when we turn from insulting a privileged group to insulting a disadvantaged and/or oppressed group.

Think about the following riddle, after you instantiate the X with the name of some ethnic or racial group that is the object of acknowledged discrimination: 'Why are Xs forbidden to swim in the Thames? They leave a ring around the harbour.' Here, inasmuch as you may worry that this sort of humour can contribute to the mistreatment or disparagement of the group in question or, at least, can encourage insensitivity to their plight, you may find this riddle morally suspect. Or think of the preceding joke about lawyers, but where the butt of the joke is some disadvantaged group.

Lawyers are well off and can defend themselves. They are strong. The minorities who are often the butt of racist and ethnic jokes are weak and vulnerable, and jokes like the preceding ones may abet their persecution either by reinforcing the pejorative stereotypes that are holding them back or by making us indifferent to the circulation of those stereotypes, thereby turning us into accessories to their oppression.

But the amoralist is ready with a response to this worry. He points out that many of the selfsame groups that are the victims at the hands of outsiders of ethnic and racist humour employ the very same comic stereotypes to themselves in their humour. The Irish, for example, tell jokes about their excessive drinking; the joke that opened the first chapter of this book could have been brokered by an Irishman (it was, in fact; I'm of Irish descent). Jewish jokes emphasize cunning, especially in matters financial. African-American jokes frequently return to the theme of voracious sexual appetites.

Similar examples can be found with respect to other groups. The American comedian Jeff Foxworthy, for example, has a routine in which he speculates upon under what conditions you could be a redneck, i.e. a poor, white, excessively clannish Southerner. For instance, he says, 'If you remarry three times and still have the same in-laws, you might be a redneck.' This is just the sort of thing a Yankee might say sincerely and derogatively about what they call poor white trash; but it's also what rednecks joke about among themselves.

Since the members of disparaged minorities employ the same stereotypes that outsiders do, the amoralist surmises that the ethnic and racist humour in question cannot constitute the sort of danger indicated above. Why would members of these groups greet these stereotypes with such glee if they were so potentially harmful to themselves?

One suggestion is that such stereotypical humour is only recruited by self-hating members of the races or ethnicities in question. But that suggests epidemics of self-loathing of such immense proportions in the relevant groups that it is strange that it is not evident in other aspects of their communal life.

Another hypothesis is that this is a class thing: the better-off members of the tribes in question mobilize these stereotypes against their less fortunate brethren. However, Shanty Irishmen are more likely to tell jokes about drunken Irishmen than the Lace Curtin Irish are. So, the amoralist surmises, the best explanation of this phenomenon is that no one takes humour to be morally serious.

Yet this suggestion strikes me as too hasty. What the amoralist overlooks is that one Jew might give a pass to another Jew telling a joke about a financially savvy rabbi, but she will not be open to a skinhead reciting with transparent malice a token of the same story type. It matters who is telling the joke and for what reason. Where the comedy is for the purpose of in-group camaraderie, as it is when an Irishman tells a story about fellow Hibernians in their cups, it will be acceptable, but when the same joke is told by an outsider in order to insult, demean, or put down the Irish, the Irishman will regard it as hurtful.

What this indicates is not, as the amoralist claims, that humour is outside the reach of morality. Rather, it shows that when it comes to evaluating humour, it important to take into account who tells the joke, in which context, and with what intention.

For example, the most common structures for delivering the kind of humour that we are discussing are highly formulaic—notably jokes and comic stereotypes. Let us call the occasions when these humour formulas are mobilized, such as the telling of a joke, joke tokens or, more broadly, humour tokens. Speaking technically, every telling—every repetition—of the previous redneck joke—is a humour token of the humour type 'If you remarry three times and still have the same in-laws, you might be a redneck.' Moreover, I claim that it is joke tokens or humour tokens that are moral or immoral, if the preceding observations about context and intentions are correct, since it will be humour tokens that are intended to be harmful. Humour types, as we've seen with respect to Foxworthy's redneck routine, can be flipped in the tokening. Thus it is the tokening that may or may not bear ill will, and, inasmuch as it is the tokening that carries harmfulness, in virtue of the harm principle, it is the tokening that is immoral or not.

Nor should it seem strange to talk about humour types and humour tokens here. When I ask you whether you've heard the one about the pig with two wooden legs, I'm inquiring whether you'd like me to token that type. Moreover, not only is it humour tokens that are moral or immoral, dependent on context and intention; it is also humour tokens that are funny or not funny, as anyone who has told a joke well on one occasion knows when she hears it bomb on another occasion when someone else tells it.

In the greatest number of cases, as represented in joke books and, nowadays, on websites, the witticisms displayed—the joke types—are recipes or scripts or, at best, loosely advisory instructions to be performed. That is why they are typically so dead on the page (or the screen). It is what the performer does with them that causes or fails to cause comic amusement. (Indeed, if you laugh at one of these joke types from the page, it is undoubtedly because you are playing a performance of it in your mind's ear either in your own 'voice' or that of a comic you admire.) Whether a humour type is effectively mobilized depends on its token execution, which relies on such performance factors as the comic's intonation and gestures (including winking) as well as such contextual information as knowing who the comic is and what she stands for (thus allowing for unmarked irony). Thus, not only is it the humour token that is moral or immoral; it is the token that is comically amusing or not.

Furthermore, inasmuch as types lack causal powers, it is the tokening of joke types in particular and humour types more broadly that can be said to cause comic amusement.

So, given the distinction between humour types and humour tokens, we can say that the amoralist is right that humour types may not be assessable as morally acceptable or wicked for the reason that the same humour type, or in this case joke type, can be advanced with different motives. What is apt for moral evaluation is the act of presenting a specific humour token with an express intention in a concrete context. For it is such acts that are potentially harmful, and therefore open to moral scrutiny.

Humour types, because they can be introduced to realize either good or evil purposes (as well as no ethically relevant purposes at all), are morally neutral. But when enlisted for immoral purposes—i.e. when mobilized with the intention to harm—their tokens can be rebuked as evil. Who can deny that a lying invocation of a demeaning ethnic stereotype for the purpose of humiliating some undeserving person in her presence is immoral?

Moreover, if, say, the anti-Semitic joke teller protests that he was only joking, we need not accept that at face value but may suspect him of occluding his true intentions. Sometimes the claim—that one is only joking—should not be taken as a sign that one is not serious, but as a sign that one is dissembling.

Yet, if amoralism is false, and it makes sense to say that at least *some* tokens of humour can be immoral, it follows that the presenter of the humour token has done something evil. But what of those who share in the appreciation of the humour token? Does laughing at a malicious sexist joke, told by a male chauvinist pig, show that one is wicked? If humour presupposes shared norms, does amusement in response to an evil joke utterance unmask us as fellow sharers in the teller's decadence? Some moralists argue that it does—that laughter at such humour necessarily discloses a sullied moral character.

Wicked laughter; evil character

A fair share of humour is malicious, dedicated to insulting its target. Many humorous presentations—including racist, sexist, and homophobic joke tokens—trade in oppressive stereotypes, reinforcing them outright or at least inviting indifference or insensitivity to their circulation, and thereby abetting unchallenged harmful and offensive libels about the groups so vilified.

Telling such jokes with the intent to hurt or harm is immoral. But rewarding such jokes with laughter, it has been argued, also makes one complicit with and thereby guilty, to some degree, of the infraction as well. For it may be argued that such laughter is symptomatic of one's commitments to the beliefs and/or to attitudes that the joke token appears to endorse—such as that this or that racial or ethnic group is exceedingly stupid, lubricious, and/or dirty.

Following a recent discussion of this topic in the literature, let us call this view the *attitude endorsement theory*. As its title signals, it is the theory that being comically amused by immoral jokes, especially those that figure in recent debates about political correctness, shows that one endorses the sexist, racist, homophobic, classist, anti-Semitic (etc.) attitudes that the jibes in question appear to presuppose. Such jokes contain an element of malice, directed at women, African-Americans, workers, gays, Jews, and so forth. The attitude endorsement theorist distinguishes the purely malicious elements in such jokes from wit, which presumably involves the simple cognitive play of things such as incongruities, and contends that laughter, or even just a smirk, indicates that you share in that unjustified malice with the teller of the tale.

The attitude endorsement theorist points out that all jokes are *conditional*; they require listeners to supply their background assumptions—in order to recognize the norms that are under fire, and to access the emotions and attitudes that the joke or cartoon presupposes in order to work. Thus, when a joke presumes malicious and immoral attitudes in order to succeed and we laugh, the attitude endorsement theorist contends that this reveals that we too are morally flawed, insofar as we share the vicious attitudes showcased in the joke.

An example that is frequently discussed in the literature as affording evidence for the attitude endorsement theory goes like this: 'M (a well-known female celebrity, widely rumoured to be sexually hyperactive) visits a hockey team. When she emerges, she complains she has been gang raped; to which the narrator responds "Wishful thinking."'

Putatively, this alleged joke relies upon a series of sexist presuppositions, including: (i) that rape is merely a variant form of allowable sexual intercourse; (ii) that many women's sexual desires are indiscriminate; (iii) that there is something objectionable about a woman who has a lot of sex. The attitude endorsement theory, in its strongest version, maintains that in order to be amused by this joke one must access all or most of the aforesaid sexist attitudes towards women, and that, if one laughs (or just snickers), this shows that one shares these attitudes—that one is, not to put too fine a point on it, a sexist.

Clearly, sexists can token joke types like this in order to cement their fellowship with other sexists. But the question is whether *anyone* who laughs at this joke is a sexist, a member of the sexist fellowship, even if he himself protests that he is unaware of this deep conviction and would deny it loudly were it suggested to him. A high-octane industrial-strength attitude endorsement theorist says 'Yes,' because he alleges that the attitudes required for uptake of this joke cannot be assumed hypothetically: they must be attitudes that compliant listeners actually share with the joke teller.

It is unfortunate that this alleged witticism has become the focus of so much discussion, since it is rather lame. Perhaps the attitude endorsement theorist has chosen it on the grounds that if you laugh at something so unfunny, the only explanation is that you bear malice towards the lady insulted by the jape (and by extension to women in general). But if this is the point—since you are laughing at something that is not comically amusing—the argument is poorly framed. That is, since the contention is that if you are *comically* amused by this invective, you manifest a bad character, then this jibe is a flawed example, because it is not comically amusing.

Also, with respect to this example, the attitude endorsement theorist is not very forthcoming about why we should take disrespect directed at one woman to generalize to disrespect for all women. Indeed, the very choice of an insult as the paradigm from which to extrapolate a theory about all humour that courts immorality, in one way or another, is, so to speak, to put one's hands on the scale, since to insult someone outright is so often patently morally offensive.

Perhaps the major problem with this particular argument for the attitude endorsement theory is that it supposes that there is only one interpretation of this joke, i.e. the sexist one that presupposes that rape is merely an acceptable variant of sexual intercourse, with no moral stigma attached. But when I first heard this joke, I did not interpret it that way. I thought that it was about hypocrisy.

M was a supposedly well-known Donna Juanita. Thus, when I first heard this joke, I thought that it was suggesting that she *had* had consensual sex with the hockey team, but then, when discovered, tried to cover it up by saying she had been gang raped—to which the sceptical narrator of the joke replies, effectively, 'Dream on, if you think we'll buy that one.' The humour, I supposed, was akin to that of unmasking a Tartuffe. That explained to me why the central character is marked as someone noteworthy for her sexual appetites.

(Moreover, the attitude endorsement theorist's interpretation does not seem completely coherent. If M had been raped and the joke assumes that rape is just a variant of sexual intercourse, what is it that she still wishes for? That is, what is the significance of the punchline 'Wishful thinking'?)

Undoubtedly, it does not help the strong version of the attitude endorsement theory that this joke is so weak (where the weakness has, in large measure, to do with the difficulty in catching on to its point). Of course, this may prompt one to adopt a weaker version of the attitude endorsement theory than the one usually discussed. On this weaker view, the idea is that if the joke is basically unfunny and you still laugh, it must be because you bear a malicious attitude towards the butt of the joke. Perhaps this is right most of the time. But it is an exceptionally diluted position. I wonder if it is even a hypothesis about humour, since it seems to amount to the claim that if the joke isn't comically amusing then our laughter must be of some other sort. Maybe it is an example of triumphant laughter. But triumphant laughter is distinct from comic laughter. Thus, the diluted version of the attitude endorsement theory doesn't seem to be about humour at all.

Maybe it doesn't make much sense to quibble over the correct interpretation of this particular joke. But there is a theoretical point here. Many jokes support a variety of interpretations, several of which may promote laughter. This is not to say that jokes are completely open texts. The interpretations generally fall within a circumscribed range. However, a joke may possess more than one reasonable interpretation, each of which may lead to laughter. In the preceding example, the target of ridicule may be female sexuality, as the attitude endorsement theorist says, or it may be hypocrisy, as I thought.

But if a non-sexist interpretation of the joke promotes comic laughter, then the attitude endorsement theorist cannot infer, as he so casually does, that anyone who laughs at the joke reveals a morally flawed, sexist character. The attitude endorsement theorist neglects the possibility that some jokes that appear on his interpretation to be sexist may be risible to others under non-sexist interpretations. Consequently, the inference pattern he proposes is inadequate.

Of course, it is often very difficult to pinpoint exactly what engenders comic laughter in a humorous exchange. It could be the propositional content of a joke, or it could just be the weird voice that the teller assumes in retailing the story. And this supplies further reason to be wary about taking someone's amusement at, for example, an allegedly sexist joke as a reliable indication of a deep-seated attitude.

As previously noted, it is also not clear what warrants the attitude endorsement theorist to take an insult directed at one particular woman to reveal an attitude towards all women. Nor does taking an insult as the exemplar of all humour seem untendentious. But these may be problems specific to this particular joke.

So let us look at an unequivocally sexist joke of the sort that the attitude endorsement theorist is hankering after—an old *Playboy* definition: rape is an assault with a friendly weapon. Does laughter at this reveal an ingrained sexist character? Many would deny it, arguing that what they laugh at is the incongruous word wit, the oxymoronic juxtaposition of disparates (assault and deadly weaponry yoked together with friendship). True, readers must in some sense recognize the sexist attitude that underwrites this nonsense. But the question is whether they have to affirm or endorse it. They might be laughing at the implied speaker of this joke—after all, they regard it as silly and nonsensical, a faux definition.

Yet even if this is too baroque an interpretation of what is going on here, still it seems plausible for the amused listener to say: I was only laughing at the word wit and I was only entertaining the notion that rape is not really grievous bodily assault, simply for the sake of accessing the wit. My laughter no more entails my endorsement of the fallacious view in question than my laughter at a crazy definition of death would show that I really feel that death is not a morally serious event.

Surely one can entertain ideas one in fact eschews for the purposes of comic amusement. Atheists, for example, can enjoy *New Yorker* cartoons about heaven or Gary Larson's *Far Side* cartoons about hell, although they believe in neither of those places. For, following Sidney again, we may say that their laughter, in other words, affirms nothing. Likewise, every adult, knowledgeable of the relevant conventions, can enjoy jokes about Santa Claus, Mrs Claus, their elves, and their airborne, red-nosed reindeer, while holding no beliefs about their existence or attitudes for or against them.

The supporter of the strong version of the attitude endorsement theory denies this possibility, maintaining that the attitudes revealed in, at least, apparently purely malicious humour cannot be assumed merely hypothetically. The attitude endorsement theorist does not really offer an argument to this conclusion. And, on the face of it, it appears counter intuitive.

In jokes, we entertain or imagine all sorts of possibilities that we do not believe: that there are genies who grant wishes, that there is an afterlife, that peanuts can talk, that death can be outsmarted. Why then is it not possible for us provisionally to imagine, incongruously, that rape is just sexual intercourse? Indeed, it is probably the very incongruity of this thought that provokes amusement, although to be amused in this way presupposes that we disbelieve it (i.e. find it incongruous) rather than affirm it. Such amusement may involve the momentary anaesthesia of the heart so common in humour, but, by the same token, it need not reveal one's true attitudes any more than momentarily entertaining an exaggerated view of Irish drinking habits or Scottish or Welsh parsimony shows a malicious attitude to real Irishmen or real Scots or Welshmen.

The attitude endorsement theorist's answer, I conjecture, is that the requisite attitudes with respect to profoundly malicious humour are not merely of the order of beliefs, but are emotionally charged and, for that reason, cannot be simply entertained, but must be deeply sedimented in one's very being. However, this seems unsubstantiated. Dumb blonde jokes appear to presuppose certain negative attitudes towards blonde women and their intelligence. Yet I can laugh at them while knowing many blonde women whose intelligence I admire. Some of these blondes laugh at them too; often they tell them to me. Indeed, many women dye their hair blonde—no gesture of disrespect there—but also enjoy blonde jokes.

The attitude endorsement theorist seems insensitive to the fact that, especially with jokes, we are dealing with a fictional genre, in which the blonde is an imaginary being and a fictional convention. Certainly, it is possible for us to entertain emotions towards fictional beings that we would not mobilize for their comparable real-world counterparts. Given the fictional context, I cheer on the imaginary ageing gunslinger but if I met up with him on the street, I would probably slink away and notify the police.

The emotions I entertain in response to fictions need not be taken as an index of my authentic attitudes. I take the blondes in blonde jokes to be a fictional convention, and I take pleasure in the clever manipulation of that convention.

Indeed, it is possible to enjoy an ethnic joke at the putative expense of some group without even having any view of or attitude towards the group in question. I laughed at a Newfie joke (How do you know a Newfie has been using your computer? There's white-out on the screen.) before I knew what a Newfie was and, even now, knowing that, I bear no animus to persons from Newfoundland. Newfie jokes are merely moron jokes, localized. Likewise, in order to avoid being called into the dean's office, I often retell as Martian jokes jokes originally told to me as Polish jokes. The students still respond with laughter (although it may be that they fear their grades will suffer if they don't laugh at my jokes).

Many of the stereotypes that worry the attitude endorsement theorist are little more than literary conventions. The blondes in blonde jokes are stock characters, as are the Newfies in Newfie jokes and the morons in moron jokes. Perhaps some people mobilize these stereotypes with hatred in their hearts, but it is hard to imagine who these people might be. Who intends harm to the moron? Maybe you will say that it is easier to identify these people when the stereotypes concern currently oppressed groups. Fair enough. But even with respect to currently oppressed groups, it is plausible that some of those who acknowledge the pronounced inaccuracy of the stereotype can still be amused by its manipulation—possibly in terms of word wit. While disbelieving it, they are able to imagine it hypothetically, in the way that the atheist accepts the existence of hell as a convention in cartoons about the devil.

That the attitude endorsement theorist neglects the role that imagination and fiction play in jokes compromises his hypothesis about vicious humour. Although such humour may serve as a vehicle for malicious attitudes—and be morally contemptible for that very reason—such cases do not support the generalization that laughter in response to predominantly politically incorrect humour always inevitably reveals an evil attitude, since the laughter may be at whatever wit resides in the joke, and the presuppositions and emotions required to access that wit may merely be imaginatively entertained and directed at fictional beings.

Moreover, jokes, even ostensibly racist jokes, are often far more complicated than the attitude endorsement theorist acknowledges. For example, there is the story about a genie who, due to their joint possession of a magic lamp, comes upon an African-American, a Jew, and a redneck. He grants each a wish. The African-American wishes that his people be returned to Africa; the Jew that his people be returned to Israel. Once the redneck realizes that the blacks and the Jews have all left America, all he wishes for is a Budweiser.

Told by a racist to racists, the joke may celebrate communal hatred; told by a liberal to another liberal, it still gets a laugh, although this time perhaps at the expense of the redneck and his very limited, monomaniacal, and warped economy of desire. The context of a joke utterance and the interpretations and purposes that tellers and listeners bring to it are crucial for assessing the ethical status of a joke transaction. The attitude endorsement theorist is too quick to assume that apparently politically incorrect jokes always have an invariant meaning and invariably elicit authentically malicious responses. But this need not be so.

Undoubtedly the attitude endorsement theorist is correct in claiming that, when a joke serves to convoke a community of genuine malice against the innocent, it is evil. But he is simply wrong in hypothesizing that every joke transaction with strong, apparently politically incorrect elements serves that purpose. Moron jokes are not usually told to commemorate or reinforce hatred for the cognitively challenged; in fact, I have never heard one told for that purpose. Rather, their conventions and stereotypes, including their stereotypical attitudes, are entertained imaginatively, rather than embraced, in order to motivate incongruities.

Much humour is transgressive. This is especially true of much recent comedy, such as that of Frankie Boyle, that seems bent upon taunting the guardians of political correctness. But the transgressiveness of American TV shows such as *The Simpsons*, *South Park*, *The Man Show*, *Family Guy*, and the late Bernie Mac's aggressive rant against children in the movie *The Original Kings of Comedy* has a double edge. Not only are 'forbidden' ideas and emotions aired, thereby engendering comic amusement through the exhibition of incongruous improprieties, but, at the same time, the attitudes underlying these transgressions may be, ironically enough, satirized.

Al Bundy's misogynistic badinage in the American sitcom *Married with Children* provokes laughter by flouting moral rules, but also pokes fun at the character himself, whose attitudes, like Homer Simpson's, are revealed to be nearly Neanderthal. Responding to such aggressive humour, then, need not signal endorsement of the attitudes displayed in the humour, but may indicate our feelings of superiority to them. And, even if in some cases we are laughing because we recognize something of Homer Simpson or Al Bundy in ourselves, our laughter may not be affirmative, since we are, in effect, knowingly laughing reflexively at ourselves as well, and in that sense hardly endorsing the hateful, potentially harmful attitudes in question.

Similarly, the outrageous views about Canadians voiced by the citizens of the American cartoon series *South Park* are really satiric reflections upon the chauvinism of US citizens. Because demeaning humour, of an ostensibly politically incorrect sort, can come replete with so many complex layers of meaning (including ironic meanings), the attitude endorsement theorist's confident conclusions about the implications of responses to the relevant sort of dismissive humour appear far too facile.

On the other hand, some humour is immoral, as we have conceded, and that entails that it is wicked. But does this imply that it is less comically amusing for being evil? According to the view called *ethicism*, it does. A specimen of humour is less funny at least to the extent that it is ethically flawed on this view, to which we now turn.

Comic ethicism

Comic ethicism is another attempt to explore the relevance of immorality to humour. Most would concur that there are, for example, immoral jokes—joke tokenings that should not be enacted and should not be encouraged. Indeed, one can conceive of an extreme form of moralism that goes so far as to claim that such joking is not even humorous—that such specimens of attempted humour are not even funny at all. That is, such joking is not only evil: it is not even comically amusing. Comic ethicism is best understood in contrast to this sort of extreme moralism.

For the ethicist, immorality does not preclude altogether the humorousness of a joke utterance. Nevertheless, immorality does always count against its humorousness. A joke utterance that contains immoral elements may also contain elements of formal wit and cleverness, and the latter may outweigh the immoral elements in an all-things-considered assessment of its humour. But even if they are outweighed, the immoral elements are *always* bad-making features of a joke utterance qua joke (or qua humour), and not merely in terms of its moral status. If a joke utterance with immoral elements is humorous overall, according to the ethicist, that is only because it contains other relevant features that counterbalance its moral blemishes. And, of course, in some situations, the immoral elements may overwhelm whatever traces of cleverness obtain; in such circumstances the joke utterance is not, all things considered, funny.

The ethicist defends this view by means of what has been called the *merited response argument*. When we judge a joke utterance to be humorous, we do not do so on the grounds that it in fact causes laughter in a certain number of people. That is, humorousness is not merely a statistical or descriptive concept. Everyone else in the room might laugh at it, but we may still judge the token joke utterance unfunny. Our judgement here is a normative one: does the joke utterance *merit* a positive response? That is, is our laughter appropriate; does the joke utterance *deserve* our laughter? Is it worthy of our amusement?

Comic amusement is a complex response to many aspects of the joke utterance—not simply to its cleverness, but also to the affect the joke summons up. And these elements can come apart. The joke utterance may merit a positive response because of its wordplay, but the affect it calls forth may be inappropriate—for instance, because it is repulsively immoral. If the negative aspects of the affective dimension are more commanding than the cleverness, then, all things considered, our positive response to the joke is unmerited (the joke utterance is not, overall, funny). If on the other hand, the cleverness is more compelling, the joke merits being called humorous, all things considered—i.e. funny—although nevertheless it is still flawed or blemished qua joke to the extent that it is immoral.

Ethicism, unlike extreme moralism, can grant that some joke utterances with immoral elements can be funny. It thereby appeals to our ordinary intuitions about the matter. But, in regarding said elements as inappropriate features, ethicism can also accommodate the possibility that there are joke tellings so thoroughly and repulsively evil that they are not truly funny at all.

The persuasiveness of ethicism depends upon the merited response argument. That argument presupposes that in order for the response of comic amusement to be merited, it must be appropriate. But to the extent that the object of comic amusement is morally flawed, the response is not merited. Nevertheless, critics of ethicism complain about the legitimacy of this conception of comic amusement.

For this conception certainly seems to be at variance with our ordinary concept of comic amusement, which, roughly speaking, seems to be thought of as a matter of enjoying certain incongruities (including moral ones). But the ethicist, in addition, requires as a criterion of appropriateness for an amused response that the humour not be morally defective. However, a *comically* appropriate response—finding something funny—does not in everyday parlance require moral appropriateness. As we have seen, it is possible to find something comically amusing while simultaneously acknowledging that it traffics in moral improprieties. Or, at least, that is the way in which we usually think about comic amusement. Ethicism seems revisionist. The ethicist appears to be importing extra considerations into the concept of comic amusement and to be treating this ramified concept of comic amusement as if it were widely shared, even obvious. In this way, the ethicist is open to the charge of equivocation.

In response, the ethicist may put their cards on the table and say outright that it is not our ordinary concept of comic amusement that is at issue but one in which the appropriateness of an amused response requires that the response be morally appropriate. But this appears to beg the question; for, then, moral appropriateness seems to be built into the very criteria of comic amusement. Yet this is what the ethicist should be demonstrating as their conclusion; they should not presume it from the get-go. Whether, for example, a joke candidate merits *comic* amusement, it can be argued, depends upon whether, with reference to the prototypical case, it engenders pleasure through its manifestation of certain incongruities—which, of course, may encompass moral incongruities.

To demonstrate that moral transgressions count against classifying a joke utterance as funny requires an argument to that result. The ethicist has not supplied such an argument; they have merely assumed what ought to be their conclusion as a premise—(or so sceptics will charge) by conflating the prima facie criteria for the appropriateness of comic amusement with the criteria of appropriateness for a response *tout court* to the joke utterance, which overall response, of course, would include considerations of moral rectitude.

If the ethicist wants to convince those who are sceptical that, in order to be funny, a joke utterance cannot be saliently immoral, the ethicist needs to share common premises with the sceptic. The sceptic will deny that to be a merited response qua *comic* amusement to a joke utterance requires that the joke be morally blameless. Comic amusement, the sceptic may say, is amoral. But in any event, the burden of proof weighs upon the ethicist. Thus, the sceptic will reject the supposition that a merited response of comic amusement must take into account the moral merit or demerit of the jest. To confuse the meritedness of the comically amused response with its moral merit is, according to the sceptic, nothing short of an equivocation.

Perhaps the ethicist's temptation to include moral appropriateness as a condition for genuine comic amusement is connected to her view that even if everyone else is laughing at a joke utterance, it is still plausible to say that the joke is not funny since, on her account, funniness is a normative judgement, not a descriptive statement. Moreover, the ethicist may ask: What could make sense of this, except that moral considerations come into play in this context?

But is it truly plausible to say that something is not really funny if virtually everyone is amused by it? Maybe being comically amused is simply a descriptive concept and not a normative one.

Of course, we do sometimes say, 'That's not funny' about something that everyone else seems amused by—perhaps when a sexist slight is advanced. Yet in these cases we may simply be voicing our moral disapproval and thereby intending to dampen our own response and those of others. However, that does not establish that the humour in question is not comically amusing for others, and even, if we are honest, for ourselves. When the kindergarten teacher tells the class clown 'That's not funny,' what she means is that it is inappropriate classroom behaviour. Classroom clowning, as I seem to remember it, was often very funny.

Maybe when it is claimed in the face of gales of laughter that 'That's not funny,' what is really being said is that others should not find it funny, although why in all cases others should not find it funny is unclear, since, as argued in the previous section, we need not be endorsing the moral incongruity in question but merely entertaining it imaginatively.

Comic immoralism

According to ethicism, a specimen of humour that is morally flawed is also supposedly unfunny, at least to the extent that it is morally defective. This is putatively a consequence of the fact that humour is a normative concept rather than a descriptive concept—that is, something can be unfunny, even if almost everyone is comically pleasured by it. This is a somewhat strange normative concept, however, since it only appears to track funniness in one direction. It assesses humour as comically defective if it is morally defective, but does not find humour funnier if it is morally inspiring. Wouldn't the merited response argument predict that more morality should make a joke more merited in terms of comic amusement, if less morality makes it less funny? Unfortunately, the ethicist never explains this asymmetry between the satanic and angelic potentials of humour, although surely it is worthy of comment. Indeed, this asymmetry may suggest to some that morality has nothing to do with funniness.

However, a deeper charge against ethicism, as we've seen, is that sceptics allege that the ethicist has begged the question by including moral appropriateness as a necessary condition for comic appropriateness. Foremost amongst these sceptics is the *comic immoralist*, who believes that ethical flaws may not detract from the funniness of a humour token but rather can enhance its comic effect.

Comic immoralism has a great deal of intuitive appeal, especially for those drawn to an incongruity theory of comic amusement. For, on that view, comic amusement is brought about by perceived incongruities of a certain sort and, obviously, transgressions of moral norms can fall into that category.

For example:

> On a planet far away from Earth, inhabited by humans, there are butcher stores that specialize in human meat. When astronauts from Earth arrive, they discover display cases featuring trays of various sorts of human brains. Mathematicians' brains cost one ounce of gold per pound; the brains of physicists also go for an ounce of gold per pound. But philosophers' brains – they cost ten pounds of gold a pound. When asked for the reason behind the difference in price, the alien butcher explains: 'Do you know how many philosophers you have to kill in order to collect a pound of brains?'

Obviously, the comic immoralist claims, the fact that this joke, incongruously enough, treats cannibalism as a morally acceptable practice in this case enhances its comic punch.

Immoralism presumably could come in at least two forms of varying strengths—strong, high-octane, fully caffeinated and unfiltered comic immoralism; and moderate, unleaded, decaffeinated immoralism. Strong comic immoralism maintains that moral transgressiveness always adds to the funniness of a humour token. Moderate comic immoralism only claims that ethical transgressions sometimes elevate the comic potentials of the high jinks in which they are incorporated.

Strong comic immoralism seems too strong, embraced by no one this side of Satan. Not even superiority theorists would appear to be committed to the view that all humour is augmented by immorality, if only because some of the laughter that such theorists prize may celebrate the superiority of virtue over vice. Think Molière: 'The duty of comedy is to correct men by amusement.' Consequently, if any sort of comic immoralism is palatable, it will be moderate comic immoralism.

Moderate comic immoralism claims that sometimes the immorality of a joke, such as the preceding joke about philosophers' brains, makes it funnier. Why think this? Perhaps the moderate immoralist thinks it is obvious, because if you subtract the immorality from the joke, it will not be so funny. Of course, if you subtract the cannibalism from the preceding joke, it won't be a joke any more either. Indeed, it won't even be a story. And, of course, a joke will be funnier than a non-story. Yet one must protest that the comparison has been rigged here.

It is not the case that what makes this joke funnier than it would otherwise be is the presupposition of cannibalism. Cannibalism is what makes this a joke. Claims about what makes a joke funn*ier* are so damnably hard to operationalize just because it is difficult to subtract elements from a humour token without destroying its comic potential altogether. So whether the moderate immoralist can produce the comparisons his position would appear to presume is at least controversial.

Yet, in addition, one wants to know whether my joke utterance must be construed as immoral. It would be immoral if it mandated our endorsement of cannibalism. However, the joke does nothing of the sort. It only asks us to entertain imaginatively the thought of a planet where academic viands are marketed and to appreciate the way in which this fiction can be manipulated wittily in order to tease philosophers playfully, as I have just done. My joke token threatens no harm. The academic abattoirs here are only an invention in the service of genial competition in the faculty lounge. The joke does not agitate for a programme of extermination. That is, it does not invite anyone to embrace something harmful, where being underwritten by a harmful intention is the crux of anything worth calling an immoral humour token.

If this joke were truly evil, it would enjoin us to believe that cannibalism is morally acceptable. And if it were to serve as a confirming instance of moderate immoralism, a token of this joke would have to be funnier when it asks us to embrace cannibalism as morally acceptable rather than when it merely asks us to imagine a planet where it is practised. But there is no evidence that any or at least many would or do find the joke funnier because they believe or believe they are mandated to believe that cannibalism is morally acceptable rather than assessing the joke to be as funny insofar as they find it to be as a result of entertaining the thought of a planet of academic butcher shops and then, in consequence, appreciating the witty faculty rivalry that such a fictional set-up affords.

Indeed, I wonder whether anyone actually finds this joke funny, let alone funnier, because it (if it does) mandates the immoral belief in the acceptability of cannibalism, instead of some other mental state, such as simply supposing hypothetically a cannibal planet where human butcher shops are kosher. The only people capable of believing cannibalism is acceptable are probably cannibals, if there are any, and they would be apt, as I would be, to be put off by these prices anyway.

Furthermore, it is worthwhile to think seriously about generalizing one way or another from this discussion. It is very hard to find examples—in fact, I know of none—where the joke is funnier because we accept the putative mandate of a joke instance to believe that something that is unethical is morally acceptable. In every case that I know of, all the comic amusement to be had from the humour token could be derived from it by imagining the fiction it presupposes and simply enjoying the incongruous complications it encourages.

Comic immoralism, even moderate immoralism, purports that evil can make an instance of humour funnier. If an instance of humour is evil, then it is because it beckons audiences to believe in the acceptability of the immorality that it broadcasts. But moderate comic immoralism provides no reason for us to agree that the humour in question would not be as funny if we merely imagined the relevant immoral practices, such as cannibalism, were the norm in the fiction. Imaginary cannibalism warrants a pass in the fiction, since there is nothing immoral about entertaining a thought such as this suppositionally or as unasserted. Thus, moderate comic immoralism fails to establish that by being apparently immoral, a token instance of humour is even sometimes funnier than it would be otherwise.

In fact, there are more grounds for hypothesizing that at least sometimes the immoral address of an instance of humour will have the effect, for standard audiences, of compromising their enjoyment of the wit. For there may be certain things that the humour asks us to entertain that our moral imaginations just resist. And this *imaginative resistance* to the immoral address of certain humour tokens may supply grounds for yet another position, which we may label *moderate comic moralism*, and which will be the last approach to be surveyed in our overview of the possible takes on the relation of morality to humour.

Moderate comic moralism

Most people, I think, would agree that at least some humour is immoral. A racist joke told with the intention to vilify in the presence of and at the expense of a member of a minority can be hurtful. That is wrong, morally. But even if the joke is told behind the backs of its targets, it may still cause harm either by reinforcing pernicious, systematic stereotypes or at least by encouraging indifference to their existence and dissemination. But can instances of telling such jokes render them unfunny, due to their blatant immorality?

The distinguished philosopher of humour Ted Cohen rejects this possibility. He writes: 'Wish that there were no mean jokes. Try remaking the world so that such jokes will have no place, will not arise. But do not deny that they are funny. That denial is a pretense that will help nothing.' Yet it seems to me that on some occasions, telling certain immoral joke tokens or advancing other forms of unethical humour tokens can diminish and even altogether extinguish the comic amusement to be had from the humour at issue. That is, the moderate comic moralist maintains that *sometimes* the immorality of a joke or humour token can render its telling unfunny, or, at least, unfunnier.

Cohen's example of a case that he believes proves his point is the following riddle: 'How did a passerby stop a group of black men from committing gang rape? He threw them a basketball.' Cohen takes this to be undeniably amusing.

In order to assess this claim, think here of the relevant joke token not as delivered by a comic such as Chris Rock, who might present it to his racial community in the spirit of bracing self-criticism, but as told by a well-known bigot to an auditorium full of neo-Nazis. Is this funny or not?

Of course, to answer this question, we must ask what is meant by unfunny (and funny) in this context. It seems that this can mean one of three things: (i) that you understand it—you recognize the incongruity or incongruities proffered; or (ii) you enjoy the joke; or (iii) you enjoy it because you understand it. I think that (iii) is the usual interpretation of finding a joke *funny*. So, finding a joke token funny is putatively thought to be a matter of enjoying it because you understand it. Here, enjoyment or pleasure is key to finding the joke token or other sort of humour token funny. However, it appears obvious that one may fail to enjoy humour—an intended racial slur, for example—just because one understands it for what it is.

A humour token requires an audience to complete it. In order to complete something such as a joke, the listener has to muster the right sort of mental state. This state may either be one of belief or one of imagining. Often with respect to ostensibly immoral jokes—such as the one involving philosophers' brains—we only entertain the thought that some immoral practice is acceptable in some fictional world.

However, on some occasions—for example, while passing by a Ku Klux Klan rally—we may hear a racist joke that calls upon us or mandates us to believe that some malicious racist insult is accurate. In such a situation, the mind of the morally conscientious listener may recoil, refusing to believe in the stereotype or even to entertain it imaginatively. In that case, the listener in question will not enjoy the joke or take pleasure from it. She will not be engaged—will not be comically amused. Her imaginative resistance here precludes her finding the joke funny, as will others of a comparable level of moral development. An actual case in point here is the representation of the African–American legislature in D.W. Griffith's film *The Birth of a Nation*, which, though intended to be comic, fails to engender amusement in (I hope) most contemporary viewers. At least it fails to move me to laughter.

Likewise, even if the humour token in question does not mandate belief in something morally noxious, it may still strain the imagination of the morally conscientious audience member to the breaking point. It may ask us to imagine something that we cannot even contemplate without experiencing a shudder of moral revulsion, where the moral revulsion outweighs or blocks the possibility of deriving pleasure from the humour token.

Considerations such as this gain plausibility by recalling that sometimes attempts at humour—involving, for example, coprophagia—can be so physically revolting that most are more likely to gag in response to it rather than to laugh. Moral revulsion can work in the same way. It may stop the imagination in its tracks and, with it, comic amusement.

Moreover, on the theory of comic amusement developed in the first chapter of this book, we can explain why at least some immoral humour may not be enjoyed. On our account, one derives comic amusement from perceived incongruities that are not anxiety producing or threatening. But clearly some immoral incongruities may produce anxiety and be threatening, if not to the listener personally, then to the greater moral order and thereby, at least indirectly, to society at large.

In some cases, the wickedness of the humour in question may be so disturbing to the relevant listeners that access to the enjoyment of the pertinent incongruity will be hindered, if not totally obstructed. Where the perceptible evil of the humour token is itself a predictable source of anxiety, it seems reasonable to conjecture that the immorality in question can contribute to the alienation of comic amusement. Sometimes, that is, owing to excessive moral outrageousness, the anaesthesia of the heart will be too difficult for an audience of moderate moral sensitivity to sustain. And they will not be amused.

Thus, contra Cohen, some immoral joking will not be comically amusing because it is recognized or understood to be wickedly motivated by righteous listeners of normal ethical sensitivity.

Of course, in many instances, audiences will not take the immorality advanced by the humour token to be genuinely threatening. Thus, many humour tokens—such as our story about the philosophers' brains—will not incur imaginative resistance and can be enjoyed, since they are not taken in earnest. After all, no one is seriously advocating that academics be added to our diets.

Similarly, some humour and its contexts are complicated enough that the evil intent they are meant to parlay flies under the audience's radar screen. A misogynous jibe, for example, may carry more hatred than the listeners grasp. So once again, in the absence of any perception of outright evil, it might be accepted imaginatively and enjoyed.

Earlier, I discussed the phenomenon of black humour. I maintained that the target of things such as dead baby jokes was not dead babies but certain grim puritanical moralizers. Those folks cannot imaginatively entertain the premises of dead baby jokes, despite their absurdity. This confirms the claim that perceived immorality can provoke imaginative resistance. But does it also indicate that black humour will not amuse the morally conscientious among us?

I don't think so. The target of such humour, as I argued in the first chapter, is not your average morally conscientious audience member. It is the moralizer—one who is excessively finicky, often with respect to objects that do not warrant moral disapprobation. He is not sensitive, but hypersensitive. Black humour is designed to reveal this flaw in his character. In doing so, it corrects the vanity and oppressiveness of extreme moralism and, for that reason, has a moral mission. Black humour is, in effect, a kind of moral immoralism.

In arguing for moderate comic moralism, I have focused on the way in which a humour token may impede or even obliterate comic enjoyment by intentionally advancing immorality in such a way as to engender imaginative resistance in morally conscientious audiences of standard ethical maturity. That is, a humour token may prevent uptake.

Some may argue that this fails to address the question of whether humour types—such as joke types and comic stereotypes—can lose their amusement potential through being morally defective. However, I wonder whether it makes sense to ask this question about humour types, since it is humour tokens that are what are funny—i.e. specific retellings of jokes, for instance—as well as what are immoral or not. Humour types, in contrast, are not determinately fixed in their moral valence as the possibility of flipping them in the tokening, among other things, demonstrated in our debate with the amoralist. And inasmuch as it is humour tokening that is pertinent here, the conclusion appears unavoidable that at least *some* humour tokens may block comic amusement because they are immoral, their immorality, in such cases, *pace* sceptics such as Cohen, compromising their funniness.

Concluding remarks

In this chapter, I have reviewed some of the relations between humour and value (including disvalue). I have argued that much of the positive value that humour accrues is due to the social function that it performs, by rehearsing and refining the norms that constitute the various cultures and subcultures to which we belong. Humour is able to discharge this service by trading in incongruities that underscore deviations from the aforesaid norms, thereby cultivating our command of those norms and reinforcing them.

Of course, humour is not always on the side of the angels. It may not always be satanic, as Baudelaire suggests, but it often serves as the devil's workshop. For example, many sexist, ethnic, racist, and homophobic joke utterances are intended to do harm. Thus, there is a connection between forms of humour and immorality. Indeed, there may be more than one relation between these humour tokens and disvalue in terms of immorality.

In this chapter, we rejected the amoralist's claim that humour is beyond good and evil, and instead argued that humour can be and sometimes is evil. This led us to ask whether the wickedness of an instance of humour makes it less amusing or more amusing. We rejected the immoralist's assertion that it can make a jest funnier and the ethicist's counter assertion that moral defectiveness always makes a humour token less funny to the degree that it is evil. In the end, we opted for moderate comic moralism, the view that sometimes an attempt at humour may be less amusing or even altogether unamusing if it mandates audiences to endorse noxious ethical beliefs, emotions, and attitudes.

However, although moderate comic moralism agrees that sometimes humour may fail to secure audience uptake due to our rejection of the comic contract the humorist extends to us, moderate moralism does not assent to the proposition that if we enjoy an ostensibly immoral specimen of humour, this reveals our character to be morally blemished. For we may be laughing at the way in which the humorist formally manipulates the various incongruities, including moral incongruities, at play in the jest, and merely imaginatively entertain them rather than endorsing or accepting them.

This has the perhaps surprising upshot that one may, for example, retail and enjoy in good conscience various ethnic jokes—such as Italian jokes, Irish jokes, Scottish, German, Dutch, and WASP jokes, etc.—at least in contemporary America. However, it is still prudent to exercise caution in this vicinity. For though one can be relatively certain nowadays that one harbours no malice towards WASPS, Irishman, Italians, and many other non-endangered ethnicities, one may not be so sure about one's feelings and actual intentions with respect to other less advantaged groups—including women, gays African–Americans, Hispanics, and Asians.

The wells of racism, sexism, homophobia, etc. run deep and are often unbeknownst to us. We may be unaware of our own unacknowledged hostilities towards various oppressed groups.

Moreover, we are also generally uninformed about the actual feelings and attitudes of the audiences to our sundry attempts at humour. Thus the most advisable guideline in this regard may be to refrain from indulging in humour at the expense of such groups insofar as we cannot be sure whether we are actually stoking hatred or, at least, insensitivity, in our own hearts and/or those of our audience towards these oppressed or at least disadvantaged groups.

So let me conclude this short introduction with a word of warning: sometimes silence is the best policy.

References and further reading

A very short introduction

N. Carroll, 'Two Comic Plots', *Art in Three Dimensions* (Oxford: Oxford University Press, 2010).

Chapter 1. The nature of humour

General introductions to humour

M. Apte, *Humour and Laughter: An Anthropological Approach* (Ithaca, NY: Cornell University Press, 1985).

A.J. Chapman and H.C. Foot (editors), *Humour and Laughter* (London: John Wiley and Sons, 1976).

P.E. McGhee and J.H. Goldstein (editors), *Handbook of Humor Research* (New York: Springer-Verlag, 1983).

P.E. McGhee and A.J. Chapman (editors), *Children's Humor* (London: John Wiley and Sons, 1980).

R.A. Martin, *The Psychology of Laughter: An Integrative Approach* (London: Elsevier Academic Press, 2007).

The Monist, Humour issue, vol. 88, no. 1 (January, 2005).

J. Moreall, *Taking Laughter Seriously* (Albany: State University Press of New York, 1983).

J. Moreall (editor), *The Philosophy of Laughter and Humor* (Albany, NY: State University Press of New York, 1987).

J. Moreall, *Comic Relief: A Comprehensive Philosophy of Humor* (Oxford: Wiley-Blackwell, 2009).

D.H. Munro *The Argument of Laughter* (North Bend, IN: University of Notre Dame Press, 1963).

M. Mulkay, *On Humor: Its Nature and Place in Modern Society* (Oxford: Blackwell, 1988).

R.R. Provine, *Laughter: A Scientific Investigation* (New York: Penguin, 2000).

The superiority theory

Aristotle, *Basic Works of Aristotle*, edited by Richard McKeon (New York: Random House, 1941).

C. Baudelaire, 'On the Essence of Laughter', in his *The Painter of Modern Life and Other Essays*, translated by Jonathan Lane (London: Phaidon Press, 1995).

F.H. Buckley, *The Morality of Laughter* (Anne Arbor, MI: University of Michigan Press, 2003).

T. Hobbes, 'Thomas Hobbes (1588–1679)', in J. Moreall (editor), *The Philosophy of Laughter and Humor*.

C.R. Gruner, *The Game of Humour: A Comprehensive Theory of Why We Laugh* (New Brunswick, NJ: Transaction Publishers, 1997).

Plato, *The Collected Dialogues of Plato*, edited by Edith Hamilton and Hamilton Cairns (Princeton, NJ: Princeton University Press, 1978).

The incongruity theory

A. Breton, *Anthology of Black Humor*, translated by M. Polizzotti (San Francisco, CA: City Lights Books, 1997).

J. Beattie, 'Essay on Laughter and Ludicrous Composition', in his *Essays on Poetry and Music* (Edinburgh, 1778).

M. Clarke, 'Humor and Incongruity', in J. Moreall (editor), *The Philosophy of Laughter and Humor*.

F. Hutcheson, *Reflections Upon Laughter and Remarks Upon the Fable of the Bees* (Glasgow, 1750).

A. Koestler, *The Act of Creation* (London: Hutchinson, 1964).

D.H. Monro, *The Argument of Laughter* (South Bend, IN: University of Notre Dame Press, 1963).

M. Martin, 'Humor and the Aesthetic Enjoyment of Incongruities', in J. Moreall (editor), *The Philosophy of Laughter and Humor*.

J. Moreall, *Taking Laughter Seriously* (Albany, NY: State University of New York Press, 1983).

V. Raskin, *Semantic Mechanisms of Humor* (Dordrecht, The Netherlands: Reidel, 1984).

R. Scruton, 'Laughter', in J. Moreall (editor), *The Philosophy of Laughter and Humor*.

S. Stewart, 'Not Quite Flying Nuns and Other Salvaged Skits', in the Arts and Leisure section, *New York Times*, 10 December 2008, p. 8.

M.C. Swabey, *Comic Laughter: A Philosophical Essay* (New Haven, CT: Yale University Press, 1961).

The release theory

S. Freud, 'Humor', in J. Moreall (editor), *The Philosophy of Laughter and Humor*.

H. Spencer, 'On the Physiology of Laughter', in *Essays on Education, etc.* (London: Dent, 1911).

R.L. Latta, *The Basic Humor Process* (Berlin: Mouton de Gruyter, 1999).

The play theory

T. Aquinas, *Summa Theologica*, translated by Thomas Gilby (New York: McGraw Hill, 1973).

M. Eastman, *The Enjoyment of Laughter* (New York: Simon and Schuster, 1936).

J. Moreall, *Comic Relief: A Comprehensive Philosophy of Humor* (Oxford: Wiley-Blackwell, 2009).

The dispositional theory

J. Levinson, 'Humour', *The Routledge Encyclopedia of Philosophy*, edited by E. Craig (London: Routledge, 1998).

J. Moreall, *Comic Relief: A Comprehensive Philosophy of Humor* (Oxford: Wiley-Blackwell, 2009).

Chapter 2. Humour, emotion, and cognition

Comic amusement as an emotion (or not)

J. Morreall, 'Humor and Emotion', in J. Moreall (editor), *The Philosophy of Laughter and Humor*.

R. Scruton, 'Laughter', in J. Moreall (editor), *The Philosophy of Laughter and Humor*.

R.A. Sharpe, 'Seven Reasons Why Amusement Is an Emotion', in J. Moreall (editor), *The Philosophy of Laughter and Humor*.

Neo-Jamesianism

J. Prinz, *Gut Reactions* (Oxford: Oxford University Press, 2004).

J. Robinson, *Deeper Than Reason: The Emotions and their Role in Literature, Music and Art* (Oxford: Oxford University Press, 2005).

Comic amusement and vital human interests

M.M. Hurley, D.C. Dennett, and R.B. Adams, *Inside Jokes: Using Humor to Reverse-Engineer the Mind* (Cambridge, MA: The MIT Press, 2011).

J. Miller, 'Jokes and Joking: A Serious Laughing Matter', in *Laughing Matters*, edited by J. Miller et al (Essex, UK: Longman Group, 1981).

M. Minsky, 'Jokes and their Relation to the Cognitive Unconscious', in *Cognitive Constraints on Communication*, edited by J. Hintikka et al (Dordrecht, The Netherlands: Reidel, 1981).

M. Minsky, *Society of the Mind* (New York: Simon and Schuster, 1988).

Chapter 3. Humour and value

Humour and the reproduction of social norms

H. Bergson, *Laughter: An Essay on the Meaning of the Comic* (Oxford: Macmillan, 1911).

T. Cohen, *Jokes* (Chicago: University of Chicago Press, 1999).

Wicked laughter; evil character

F.H. Buckley, *The Morality of Laughter* (Ann Arbor, MI: University of Michigan Press, 2003).

R. DeSousa, *The Rationality of Emotion* (Cambridge, MA: The MIT Press, 1987).

Comic ethicism

B. Gaut, 'Just Joking', in *Philosophy and Literature* 22 (1998), pp. 51–68.

B. Gaut, *Art, Emotion, and Ethics* (Oxford: Oxford University Press, 2006).

Comic immoralism

A. Eaton, 'Rape and Ethics in Almodovar's *Talk to Her*', in *Talk to Her*, edited by Anne Eaton (London: Routledge, 2008).

D. Jacobson, 'In Praise of Immoral Art', in *Philosophical Topics* 25 (1997), pp. 155–99.

Moderate comic moralism

A. Smuts, 'The Joke is the Thing: *In the Company of Men* and the Ethics of Humour', in *Film and Philosophy* 11 (2007), pp. 49–66.

A. Smuts, 'Do Moral Flaws Enhance Amusement?' in *The American Philosophical Quarterly* 46, 2 (2009), pp. 151–63.

A. Smuts, 'The Ethics of Humour: Can Your Sense of Humour be Wrong?' (forthcoming).

Index

D

E

F

G

H

I

J

Humour

SOCIAL MEDIA
Very Short Introduction

Join our community

www.oup.com/vsi

- Join us online at the official Very Short Introductions **Facebook** page.
- Access the thoughts and musings of our authors with our online **blog**.
- Sign up for our monthly **e-newsletter** to receive information on all new titles publishing that month.
- Browse the full range of Very Short Introductions online.
- Read **extracts** from the Introductions for free.
- Visit our library of **Reading Guides**. These guides, written by our expert authors will help you to question again, why you think what you think.
- If you are a teacher or lecturer you can order inspection copies quickly and simply via our website.

Visit the Very Short Introductions website to access all this and more for free.

www.oup.com/vsi

ONLINE CATALOGUE
A Very Short Introduction

Our online catalogue is designed to make it easy to find your ideal Very Short Introduction. View the entire collection by subject area, watch author videos, read sample chapters, and download reading guides.